AF869312

YES You Can

Make Money As An ARTI$T

A Non-Fiction Memoir
Written & Illustrated by

Warren Cullar

Figure 1: Warren Cullar "By A Nose"
Cast Bronze Sculpture, 4'x5'

Copyright © 2018 by **Warren Cullar**

All rights reserved. No part of this publication may be reproduced, distributed or transmitted in any form or by any means, without prior written permission from the author.

Warren Cullar/Cullar Gallery, Inc.
12102 Conrad Rd Austin, TX 78727
www.artwarren.com

Book Layout © 2014 BookDesignTemplates.com
Book Cover © 2018 Brian Huculak - huc .: creative LLC

Yes You Can Make Money As An Arti$t
Warren Cullar – 1st ed.
ISBN Print **978-1-7320740-0-2**
ISBN ePub **978-1-7320740-1-9**
Publisher: Cullar Gallery, Inc
Publication Date: February 28, 2018

Dedicated to Loren Taft Cullar

Figure 2: Dad reading on the south porch, 1968

"Good fortune is what happens when opportunity meets with planning."
Thomas Alva Edison

Contents

Introduction

Miss French was my first-grade teacher who told her class the timeless story of "The Little Engine That Could." She stood on a chair, moving her arms making choo-choo train sounds saying, "I think I can, I think I can, I think I can." I felt like the Little Engine (Figure 3). I was so little Mother had to produce my birth certificate to prove I was six years old to be allowed to enroll in the first grade (Figure 4). During my school years, I was constantly told I was too short, not smart enough, can't spell, can't write, shouldn't consider trying to go to college and later, "you can't make a living as an artist".

Figure 3: Little Engine That Could

Figure 4: Warren, Bonnie Blue, & Janet
First Day of School 1948

Growing up, Father was a wonderful inspiration. He taught me to work hard. His honorable and spiritual life-style inspired me to imitate him. At 18, Dad sent me out into the world as a disciplined, hardworking young man with strong values and a book. When he presented me with the book he said, "Warren, study the book, find the secrets and apply them to your life." I left home driving a 1949 Chrysler and $350. After a depressing struggle to start an independent life, I read the book. This book is the foundation of the power of positive thinking.

My book is not about artistic technique. It is a series of flashbacks highlighting peak emotional moments. To tell you about learning to draw would be boring, but to tell you why Mother used green paint to obliterate my hand painted mural on the den wall is certainly more interesting. In college, sex and embezzlement sent me down a rabbit hole I managed to escape, only to marry the wrong woman. Years later, I fell in love for the first time, marrying the right woman for love.

Writing this creative non-fiction memoir has been an adventure. I read family letters and browsed through old black and white photos of people I sometimes remember. A few I would rather not recall. To the best of my ability, this is what happened and when. The stories are written first from my experiences and second, so I could perhaps inspire other creative people who want to be successful entrepreneurs. Most of the names have been changed to protect the guilty and the innocent to insure no one will be lawsuit happy.

Your interests may range from business and engineering to the arts. If you have a burning desire to make a living as an independent entrepreneur, please take the risk! Plunge in! When you stumble or fail, do so quickly. You can always begin again with better plans. Continue to refine your work until you reach your goal and succeed.

Happily, like Sinatra's song, I did it "My Way". If I had listened to Mother, friends and counselors, I would have lived an unfulfilled life, including their type of "security" with a gold watch at retirement. For over 40 years, I've not had a boss, nor anyone to score my performance, save myself, my wife (and perhaps my collectors). I never had the fear of a pink slip in an employee mailbox. I am Captain of my life and fate. I work and play each day as I have planned. My passion as an artist is my willingness to explore. I never "do work" in the dull, mechanical sense of the word. I've made mountains of mistakes, lost money, time and a marriage, yet I keep jumping from one lily pad to another, reaching for the "Golden Ring" of prosperity. I'm not famous, but I've lived fully as an artist, earning my living for over 40 years. My art and I have succeeded when everyone said I couldn't. "I did it my way" creating and selling art. One day I discovered I was living a successful and prosperous life (Figure 5). "I think I can, I think I can," became, I DID."

Figure 5: I think I can, I think I can, I know I can, I DID!

◈ CHAPTER ONE ◈

A Saved Book

"The strength of who you are depends upon the decisions you make."
Dad

The grocery cart's metal handle was sizzling hot as I pushed a week's load of supplies to the car. Unlocking the car, I looked up at the foreboding gray-green clouds in the distance and frowned. I thought I was stepping on chewing gum, but it was the repaired soft spots of the asphalt parking lot on a hell-of-a-hot August afternoon in Austin, Texas. Even with the car windows cracked, we were opening an oven. "Donna you start the car, I'll unload the cart." Dumping a bag of ice into our Styrofoam cooler, I unloaded the cold food, grabbed a handful of ice, held it to my neck and slid into the seat. I exclaimed, "Damn! The seat's hot." I liked the "glass bubble" and sleek lines of our AMC Pacer (Figure 6), but it was like a greenhouse and made me secretly wish for the massive visor in my old 49 Chrysler.

The humidity was so intense my shirt stuck to me and Donna complained that her bra was soaking wet. She said, "I'm going to drive to that shade." She parked under the trees at the rear of the shipping dock. The car was starting to cool. We were quiet, except for the roaring air conditioner.

We were young in 1976, I was 34 years old, Donna was five years younger. She slurped the last of her Coke with only a hint of ice left. I watched her. She was pretty and healthy with long hair tied in a pony-tail. A few wisps of escaped hair were pasted to her forehead from perspiration. I smiled at her. She smiled back and said, "Ready to go?" She eased the car around to the front of the building toward the street.

Figure 6: AMC Pacer

I relaxed as the car continued to cool and cleaned my sweat covered glasses. She screamed, "Look," pointing to the horizon. I jerked up to see a dark finger-size rope of clouds, disappearing behind the trees miles away. It took a second to recognize what I was seeing, yelling, "It's a tornado let's get home!" Donna swerved into the merging traffic.

She gripped the steering wheel and glared at the ribbon of asphalt speeding toward us at 60 mph. Glancing up I said, "We're in for a storm." She nodded her head in the direction of a distant, white anvil cloud climbing to the altitude of 40 or 50 thousand feet. Her relaxed expression from sitting in the shade and letting the car cool had changed. I asked, "Are you ok?" She replied, "I just want to get home." Rolling down the window, the fresh smell of rain on hot asphalt triggered memories from childhood. I used any excuse to go outside during summer storms to splash in the gutter and collect earth worms.

We were in a tunnel of sunlight with the sky ahead of us growing darker. Watching a line of black ominous clouds rush to cover the sky northeast of our place, we both felt an urgent need to be home. My fingers fumbled with the radio. The reception gave us cursory reports of hail and lightning to the north. At Steward Junction, with only nine miles to go, we turned west. I said loudly, "I think the safest place will be in the new studio, too many windows in the house." Two months prior, we purchased a 1902 farmhouse and abandoned restaurant near the highway, east of the tiny community of Bertram, Texas. The restaurant, our future studio/gallery, would be our storm shelter.

The sky was growing darker. Rain drops the size of fried eggs plopped on our windshield as we pulled into our drive next to the porch. I yelled, "I'll put the groceries on the porch and you start taking them to the kitchen. I'll put the car up." I drove into the garage and made a dash for the porch. The pea size hail pelted me, pinging as it hit glass or metal. In the hall closet, I pulled out two old Marine Corps jackets, a flashlight and a couple of blankets. I met Donna in the kitchen with hastily made sandwiches, a thermos of water and a pillow. Her wide-eyed expression spoke fear. We went out on the long porch that ran the entire length of the house. I struggled to cover us with a blanket. The wind was loud, I had to yell, "Hold on to my belt." Donna's hand grasped my belt. We hugged our provisions and stepped off the porch into the wrath of the storm. The rain was cold and stinging, coming in sheets at a steep angle. The hundred feet or so to the studio felt like a mile with only the blanket to protect us. We moved like an undulating Chinese Dragon celebrating the New Year, sloshing our way into the studio.

I flipped on the ceiling lights, illuminating the dismal atmosphere of our furniture and still unpacked moving boxes. We dried off and began to organize our storm shelter in the narrow hall-way leading to the bathrooms. I found a box marked camping gear and to my delight, pulled out sleeping bags and spread them in the hall-way. The lights flickered. Stopping and looking at one another, we quickly piled our pillows, flashlight, and thermos of water in our hall shelter. The wind died down, the storm subsided, and the sky was filled with ominous clouds. Only a gash of distant sunlight broke the darkness. The rain retreated to a light sprinkle. Trees that had been arching and bending against the approaching storm were now delicately swaying.

Leaving the hallway, we opened the curtains, moved a few boxes and sat at our wooden picnic table to watch the storm. Donna spread our meager dinner on the paper sack. Two sandwiches, a pack of chips, and a thermos of water never tasted so good. I opened the studio door to a blast of cold air and the freshness of rain. We watched a serpentine silver stream of water run down the center of our driveway. I felt compelled to find where the cloud formations were to the North. Turning to Donna, "I'll be back shortly." She yelled back, "Don't be gone long."

Walking briskly, to see past our big trees, the wet grass quickly soaked my jeans. The experience reminded me as a kid of those neighborhood folks who scurried like mice to hide during storms. The boiling clouds were hanging dangerously low and starting to slowly swirl. I yelled, "Oh,

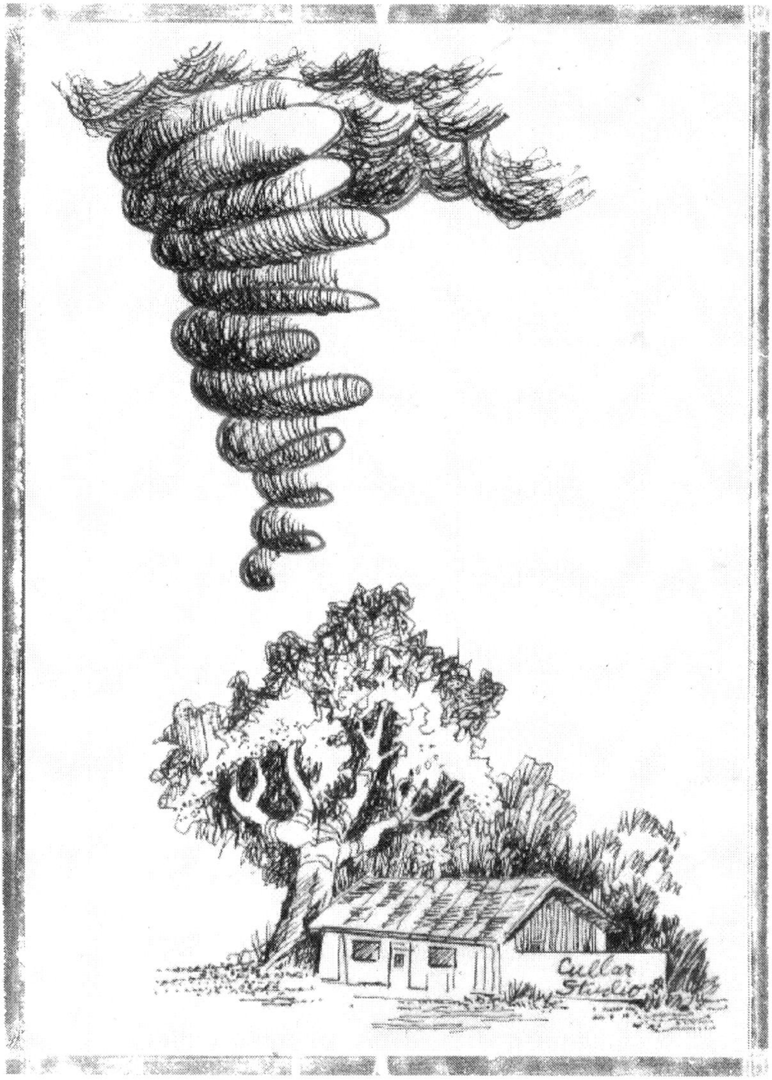

Figure 7: Bertrum, Texas, Storm Over Studio, 1976

Hell!" I turned and ran for the studio. At the same moment, an explosion violently shook the earth causing me to jump straight up, clawing at the air. A terrible sound blasted over the studio roof. Like fourth of July sparklers, a shower of electric sparks were erupting from the highway transformer. The pungent odor of burning rubber wafted through the air. The lights went out in the studio. A massive gust of wind slammed me in the chest. My heart was beating in my throat. Squinting and covering my face, feeling for the wall, I elbowed my way to the front of the studio (Figure 7).

The grinding sound of metal being torn from the roof of the house was deafening. Blindly, I groped for the studio door handle. The wind sent the aluminum screen door slamming into the side of my head. I managed to push open the jammed wooden door. In that instant, the storm hit the other side of the building, sending me sprawling across the linoleum floor. Shards of broken glass exploded in all directions. The flimsy curtains were flapping horizontally in the wind.

Stunned, I yelled, "Donna, are you alright?" She screamed, "I'm ok!" "Donna, turn on the flashlight." She yelled back, "It doesn't work." With the window gone, rain and hail were pouring in, carried by the screaming wind. The light outside was inky blue, pierced by lightning strikes that illuminated the pitch-black interior of the studio. Our studio was a surreal gothic landscape. Lightning gave me a moment to see where to walk.

I yelled at Donna, "I've got to cover the window." The glass crunched as I moved slowly through the jungle of boxes and furniture. I was confused and terrified while trying to come up with something to cover the hole where the window had been. I found several scraps of plywood but all of them were too small. The antique bookcase to the right of the blown-out window would stop the rain. Positioning my leg against the back wall, using all my strength,

I forced the bookcase into place. Moments later the soggy curtains hung limp as rain ran down the back of the case. My temple was pounding from the screen door. I felt something trickling down my neck and onto my t-shirt. I tasted the end of my finger. Blood! The lightning reflected off of the floor. I bent down, carefully picked up a handful of melting hailstones and held the ice to my bleeding temple.

My treasured books were soaking up the storm. With the next burst of light, I could see the books and quickly stuffed my favorite one under my shirt.

Donna screamed, "Warren!" I yelled back, "I'm on my way!" In the dimness, I navigated through a tangle of debris to the hall. In the blackness Donna, grabbed me yelling hysterically, "I don't want to die, I don't want to die." The staccato pounding from the hail on the metal roof, the screaming wind and lightning, were too much for her. She was losing control. I pulled her down onto the sleeping bags and hugged her tightly. The storm raged on. Time slowed to a crawl. We felt the storm would never end, but eventually it abated. Only a light rain remained; dripping off the roof.

Donna relaxed as I positioned an arm under her head. I rearranged the hastily made pallet making us a little more comfortable. In our dark clenched embrace among bedrolls, quilts and pillow, we whispered like kids playing "fort" under the dining room table. We thanked God to be alive. Exhaustion and warmth eventually took over. My temple had quit bleeding, leaving in its place a throbbing headache. The cocoon of blankets and bedrolls became cramped. When I turned over, Donna said, "What's that sharpness?" I said, "It's a book, the only one I saved from the storm." I pulled it from under my T-shirt and propped the book against the wall. I heard her sleepily mumble,

"Really, must have been special, to have saved that book…"
I whispered, "That book changed my life."

"The value of decisions depends upon the courage required to render them. The great decisions, which served as the foundation of civilization, were reached by assuming great risk, which often meant the possibility of death."
Mr. Hill

◈ CHAPTER TWO ◈

Breaking My Plate

"A good day is a planned event and thought about."
Dad

"Boys! Boys!" The voice of Dad boomed down the hall (Figure 8). The reaction was the same as it had been since I could remember: Awake! I moved under the covers, rolled over, sat up and rubbed the sleep out of my eyes. At eighteen, I still obeyed the voice that only had to say "boys" twice to know that it's time to be up and getting ready for breakfast. As a high school senior, I looked forward to graduation, though I had no major plans. I sat on the edge of the bed, looking out the window at my 1949 blue Chrysler. The 11 year old "new" car, purchased last fall, cost an entire summer working in the family air conditioning business in Abilene, Texas. One of the jobs was installing ductwork inside roofs in 100 plus degree heat, but not today. It was March and summer was a million miles away. Brother Charles was still asleep across the room. I stage whispered, "Charles, get up, it's time for breakfast." He turned over. Charles was still working at midnight in the garage on one of his cars, but this morning, as usual, Dad was calling us.

Figure 8: Warren's Dad, Loren Taft Cullar

My "little" brother, was two and a half years younger. We were very different. He spent time reading "Popular Mechanics" magazine and tinkering with anything mechanical, old cars, old TV's. I collected fossils, made drawings and worked outside with Dad in the heat, while Charles worked for a supply company as a stock boy inside a cool building. I was putting on socks when Dad appeared at the door. He noticed Charles still in bed but said nothing – very unusual. Dad was dressed in his starched blue work shirt and matching trousers with our company emblem on the flap of his left pocket. His wavy black hair had hints of white beginning at the temples and his strong jaw and stocky frame distinguished him as mature and handsome. He looked at me, smiled and asked, "Ready for breakfast?" I said, "Yes, sir."

In the kitchen, the left-hand bottom broiler of the old stove banged loudly when opened, but the aroma of cinnamon toast on a cold morning made that sound seem heavenly. Our family's kitchen was right out of a 1950 Sears and Roebuck catalog. The wall color was a pale green with a white refrigerator and a big white porcelain four burner gas stove. The yellow glass-topped table with curved chrome legs had four matching chairs with upholstery in green plastic. The kitchen also had a patterned Formica counter and linoleum floor with the look of sprinkled confetti. Two ceramic wall lamps of painted fruit hung on opposite sides of the kitchen; they were always on, as was the large ceiling light, keeping our kitchen as bright as an operating room.

All family members sat in their respective places. Charles and I sat opposite each other. When Dad wanted the attention of Charles or me, he would look us straight in the eye and tell us what he wanted us to hear. Dad was an honest man who lived by the Golden Rule. His conservative lifestyle created a family of two devoted parents and two cherished sons. Love was dished out like ice cream and looking back I want to lick the spoon of those memories. His pleasant nature, strong work ethic and spiritual values created a burning desire to emulate him.

I walked into the kitchen, said good morning to Mother and sat down. I noticed my ceramic plate and the quarter size chip on the edge, it was different from the normal, pale yellow, plastic melamine we had been using for years - very unusual. Dad was always in a hurry for his first cup of coffee. He had the habit of pouring the boiling coffee into his saucer and blowing it to cool it down to a drinkable temperature. He would then pour it back into his cup to drink.

Mother acted nervous. It was not like her to fret over breakfast. She was in control of her domain, a strong, well organized, loving woman whose enemy was dirt. Cooking was not her major talent, but she could make meals in an instant and the can opener was her best friend. Dad was always talkative in the morning, but today he looked straight through me over his saucer of cooling coffee. He was pondering, not speaking. Again, very unusual. I talked about the Spanish class trip to Saltillo, Mexico, after graduation. I had been selected to drive my car with four students. I was excited, but Dad was only partly listening. Something else held his attention. Charles appeared in the doorway, hair uncombed, shirt untucked, looking very sleepy. Mother noticed his disheveled appearance and said nothing - unusual.

Our family's kitchen table, the center of our universe, was also where everything was discussed, with a prayer and a lengthy breakfast. This morning during Dad's prayer, he stumbled with uncomfortable word choices - very unusual.

Charles took a bite of toast as Dad told him he was proud of his ability to work on cars. He said it reminded him of working on bicycles when he was Charles' age. He turned and again congratulated me for winning a city design contest for a fountain. The fountain would be installed by the city at the intersection of 1st and Pine. He asked, "Warren since you seem to have a budding ability in designing things, do you think you might pursue that study?" I shrugged my shoulders and said, "Maybe." Breakfast was finished. Mother disappeared into their bedroom. Charles went to get ready for work. I stood up from the breakfast table. Dad motioned for me to sit back down and grasped my forearm more strongly than ever before. His face was dead serious. His words were decisive, telling me how much he and Mother loved me. He hesitated for a moment and said he was proud of the man I had become and was sure I would succeed in life. He believed in me. I will never forget the next few moments. What he did changed my life forever. He reached across the table; picked up my plate and moved it off the table. He looked me in the eyes for a moment then deliberately dropped the plate. It exploded (Figure 9)! Shards went everywhere. I jumped then stared wide eyed into his face. He had a calm expression and said, "Warren, I have broken your plate at my table."

He stood up, walked to the pantry, picked up the broom and dust pan and handed me the pan. I placed it on the floor as he swept up the broken pieces. I reached behind the chair and picked up a couple of shards. I didn't know what to say. I stared at him as he put the trash can down. I emptied the dust pan. Immediately, I remembered one of his stories about "breaking the plate". It was about his uncle who told his two sons he was breaking their plates, meaning they were considered grown and on their own. I didn't have to ask what Dad meant, I knew and felt the urgent need to know the next steps. Somewhere inside a little voice screamed in panic, "What am I going to do?"

Dad said, "Warren, get ready, we'll discuss your options

as we work this morning." Saturday, was a work day with Dad in our air conditioner shop. In the bathroom, blindly staring at my reflection in the mirror, I looked worried. I was worried. I absently mindedly shaved. I was rolling in a tidal wave of thoughts and felt trapped in the undertow. Under my breath I mumbled, "What am I going to do?" I now understood his comment about the award and about studying design. The reality of Dad's announcement was dramatically starting to take effect. I didn't have a place at the family table. I felt like a jackrabbit scared up by a dog. I was running, confused and alone, not sure which way to go.

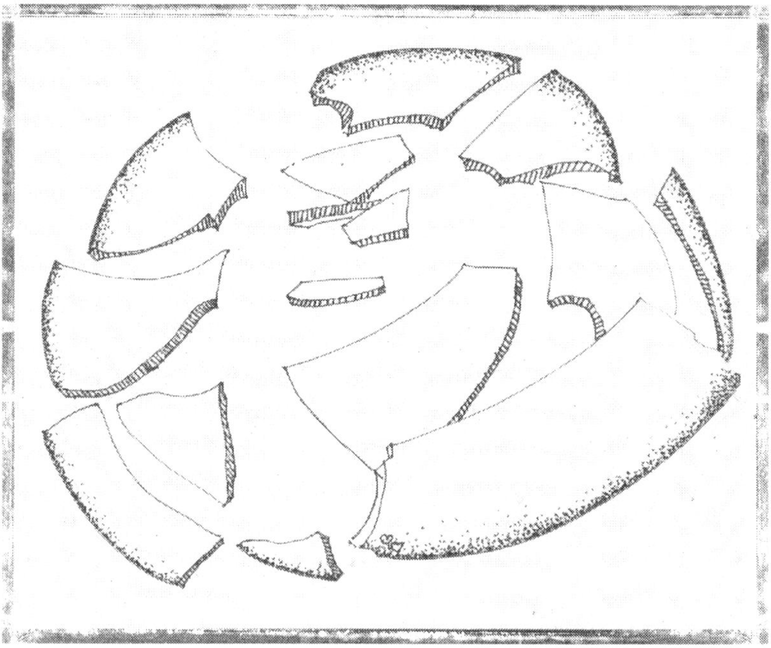

Figure 9: Warren's Broken Plate

Over the past year or so he had encouraged me to make my own independent decisions. In Dad's eyes, I was grown, loved and now considered a man. I needed to make my way in the world. I pushed open the back gate and walked across the alley where we had built our shop three years earlier. I hadn't planned beyond graduation. Now, in the still of this early morning, it was time to plan. The only sound was the crunching of my footsteps on the gravel drive. The air carried the smell of honeysuckle, accompanied by the buzzing of honey bees, each wing beat announcing spring was pushing Nature to engage. Dad was waiting. I walked in the back door of the shop. He slapped me on the shoulder. "Ready?" I managed a weak smile. We would have time to talk about the future because we were in our slow season, repairing used evaporative coolers to sell next summer.

"The starting point of achievements is desire and
the influence of that desire on your entire thinking
can motivate one to move or change the present
moment into something new and exciting."
Mr. Hill

CHAPTER THREE

The Gift

"Son, study this book and learn to apply its secrets and you will have a successful life."
Dad

At twelve I started mowing the grass with a push mower that would chop the grass in the whirling blades. Other jobs were sweeping up Dad's evaporative air-conditioning shop, stocking the shelves, and pulling apart the bales of shredded Aspen wood for Mother to make air conditioner pads.

The first day of Christmas vacation, Mother and I waited patiently outside an old warehouse in our two door Studebaker that had rust spots around the door handles and fenders. The bright cold winter sun reflected off the walls, the façade an assortment of different colors. I could read parts of a sign, "Best" and "Closin" in the faded peeling paint. A new car pulled up, the driver nodded a welcome. He was a thin man with a large Adam's apple and gray hair, carrying a cardboard box and a paper sack. Selecting a key from a key ring dangling from his belt he opened the door. I followed Mother and the owner inside to the small office. He shut the door and turned on the florescent light that instantly made an electrical buzzing sound like a thousand cicadas on a summer day. The light drooped from the ceiling at a slant.

The tall man ducked as he placed the box and sack on an old kitchen table covered with dried paint. A quick slit from a yellow handled pocket knife cut the tape on the box of a new electric heater. He plugged it in. From the paper sack, he produced two new paint scrapers and a box of one hundred single edge razor blades. He and Mother talked. Their conversation was about how he wanted to make his recently acquired warehouse better for his employees. They reached an agreement and he left. I found a couple of rickety wooden chairs and pushed them under the table. Now we had a place to take a break and eat lunch. Hopefully the heater would warm the office by the time we wanted to stop and defrost. I was anxious to explore the place. The building reeked of loneliness, a foreboding, big, empty place. The only sounds were the low cooing from the pigeons perched on the rusty metal beams. The eerie light penetrating the paint splattered windows was dull and lifeless. There were four rows of windows, dozens of them. The concrete floor was cracked and broken from many years of use. In the corner was a pile of empty cardboard boxes with a thick, cinnamon like, coating of fine dust. I walked to the back of the building. The truck size sliding metal door had an invasion of Greenbrier vines that had found an opening, grown in and died in a dull, brown, thorny tangle.

I would spend the holidays using a paint scraper (Figure 10), cleaning windows. I was 13 years old, wearing red fuzzy ear muffs and a cap. The metal head bands on the ear muffs were adjustable and always snagged my hair. Brown cotton gloves, two sweaters and an old coat provided warmth. Mother showed me how to thread a razor blade

Figure 10: The paint scraper is framed in my studio reminding me to work smarter, not harder.

into the scraper. We started in the closest corner and I used a two-step ladder to reach the bottom windows. Mother would scrape the top two rows. The wooden ladder was short and wobbly but in a few minutes, I had mastered the wobble and was scraping away. The instructions were to scrape the paint and dust that had collected on each 10" x 8" pane of glass. I boldly asked Mother, "How much are we going to make?" I can still remember her voice as she said loudly, "One thin dime a window." I was proud to work for those dimes, helping our family buy Christmas presents. Growing up I didn't feel poor, we just didn't have anything extra. We made do. I remember wearing "hand-me-down" clothes and talking about how much things cost.

By my fifteenth summer I was doing "man's work", such as air conditioning service and odd jobs. With more responsibility, I was encouraged to open a bank account. Previously, I worked for an allowance, now I earned seventy-five cents an hour. Scouting was where I excelled. In May of 1957 I was awarded the highest honor in Scouting; the rank of Eagle Scout (Figure 11).

Figure 11: Charles Cullar admires his brother's Eagle Scout badge.

At sixteen, I took the driver's license test and now needed a car. On Saturdays, we would start at six in the morning. Dad put me to work shoveling powdered concrete and sand into an old, loud, rattling cement mixer. The mixer's gears gnawed at the cogs as the rotating bucket swallowed every shovel full. My job was to keep the cement drum going all day and into the evening. We had to finish the I-beam before the cement hardened. Dad and I, plus two workers were finishing the building of the new shop across the alley from our home. We finished the construction over the next few weeks and Dad was very excited to open his new business. I was proud to be working for Dad.

Graduation was in May, the plan was to work until fall and leave in early September for Lubbock, Texas to enroll in the school of architectural engineering at Texas Tech. Dad's seasonal business was winding down, so I found one more job before September. It was a stinky job few wanted at the city dump. My nostrils flared as I tried not to breathe the acrid stench of the smoldering heaps of garbage. I turned into the wind to catch a breath and shake off the smell surging through my nostrils and filling my lungs. My hammer clawed at another nail and the sound of rust scraping against dry wood screamed for a quick moment. The nail free wood was tossed onto a growing pile. Removing my gloves, I looked at my fingers; one throbbed to the touch where a nail had caught it, but I would work until five. Each hour added to my meager bank account. Bending down to re-tie my bootlace, holding my hurt finger out of the way, I noticed coffee grounds, a half-eaten slice of pizza and cereal boxes crushed into the blades of an electric fan. These were the throw away's of society. Back aching, I bent down and pulled out another scrap board and extracted the nails. Day three ended, I had finished cleaning a mountain of lumber to be used in construction. At 4:30 pm the battered truck arrived, the lumber was loaded, and I would follow the truck out the dump gate.

Washing up for supper meant taking a hot bath to wash away the foul, disgusting odor. With clean clothes and the day's work bathed away, I devoured with canine savagery Mother's tenderized beef cutlet, mashed potatoes and canned green beans. After supper, I laid down on the half-bed feeling the knobby green bedspread. I relaxed into the softness of the mattress. Staring at the ceiling, still weary from days of pulling nails, I thought about the day I would finally leave.

Figure 12: 1949 blue Chrysler

After the summer's heat wave, the fresh hint of fall filled the air. The South porch collected autumn leaves, now starting their yearly descent from the Sycamore trees lining our street. The Autumn wind swirled the dry brown leaves round and round. They made raspy scratching sounds as if taken from a B-rated Halloween movie. That familiar sound was etched in my memory from past autumns.

The chrome-loaded Chrysler (Figure 12), which had taken a summer of sweaty work to acquire, proudly sat in the driveway. The mammoth trunk swallowed everything I brought out of the closet: Two arm-loads of clothes, a box of odds and ends from the kitchen, boots, flashlight, large Texas flag, a compass, a green and red metal first aid kit from scouting days and a small Brownie camera. Before he joined the Army, the guy across the street, gave me a well-worn 33-rpm record player, several albums of piano concertos and a sport coat, a little too large.

With the last load finished, my side of the closet was empty. I pulled the old tennis shoe lace attached to the light switch in the top of the closet, turned around, and looked at the plastic bedroom clock. 12:23 pm. I stopped, sat down on the edge of the bed and stared out the window. The middle window pane had a small round hole in the lower right-hand corner where Charles, some years before, had accidentally fired a round from his .22 caliber rifle. Knowing him, it probably wasn't an accident.

Strange what we focus on when we are about to leave. The moment I put the key in the ignition, I would be driving into an unknown future. Jell-O, that's what I was; shaking inwardly with no direction and no solidity. I sat on the edge of the bed running my fingers over the bedspread. It was an old a habit of mine. I clasped a drafting set. Each compass and pen fit snuggly into its assigned green velvet impression. Mr. Goldberg, who owned the pawn shop on Butternut Street, had charged a hefty price of four dollars for the set, used but not abused. A small borrowed drafting table was placed behind the driver's seat. Everything was packed and ready to leave the only home I had ever known.

The plan was to study architectural engineering. I had excelled in drafting classes and won an award for a fountain design. My daydreaming ended with a slight jolt bringing me back to reality. Lunch finished, I checked for anything I might have missed. I walked into the small room we called a den leading to the porch. On the stucco wall measuring 4' x 10' was a painting. In Mrs. Henigan's art class I had learned the basics of painting and had incorporated those principals into my Western landscape. I was proud of my painting. I didn't realize my art project would be the start of a lifelong career. It was also the last time I would see my largest work. Walking out on the porch, Mother followed me. She placed her hand over her eyes to shield the sun-light and smiled. I gave her a hug and a kiss on her soft cheek, and said, "I love you." She said, "Be careful" and with a kiss, handed me a paper bag filled with a chicken sandwich, chocolate chip cookies and fruit.

Mother was conservative to the core and so afraid of life, a true introvert. She was a good caregiver but had too much pride and control to allow anything in the family to be different. We did not agree on much. Although I obeyed and loved her, we were never in sync. She was concerned and wanted me to get a local job, anything with job security. If I had done what she wanted, life would have been very different. I had the desire for something better. I slowly backed into the street. We waved goodbye. She stood in the driveway, her hand extended and then she was out of sight in the rearview mirror.

Minutes later, I pulled into a gravel parking lot and saw Dad, crowbar in hand, pulling nails from a century or older corrugated metal roof. He had secured a bid to tear down an old broom factory and sell all the metal and other items. He would get a nice price at the scrap yard for the materials. Seeing me, he waved and started making his way down the rusty roof. At the bottom of the ladder he stepped off the last rung, pulled off his glove and extended his hand. The gesture of removing one's glove goes back centuries when men in battle dress removed their glove from their fighting arm as a sign of friendship. This gesture also included raising the visor on their helmet, the source of today's salute. We shook hands, hard. He slapped me on the back and motioned me to follow him into the bowels of the old structure he was bringing down piece by piece.

Sitting on a couple of old wooden beer barrels, he turned to find his ever-present thermos of coffee and unscrewed the small plastic red handled cup. He poured the still steaming liquid without offering to share. The taste for coffee would not be acquired until I joined the Marine Corps a few years later. Some small talk was exchanged and, as always, he settled back, looked at me, assessing the situation. He said, "Son, this is hard work and there is nothing wrong with that. Good honest work never hurt anyone."

I could tell by his tone, body language and the way he was holding his coffee, that he had spent considerable time thinking and composing this speech. I visualized him on the back porch, meditating on this moment, maybe weeks or even months ago. What was it he wanted to say? What final farewell words would he choose so carefully to make us both accept what was ending and what was beginning? Nothing in our world was going to alter what had started with the breaking of my plate. I would be charting the life of Warren the moment I said good bye.

He sipped his coffee. I looked past him. The old building was a mixture of stillness and silence. The sunlight was shining through the gaps in the board walls, catching the floating particles that filled the dust covered interior. I reached out to touch him on his left shoulder. "Dad..." he stopped me as if he already knew what I was about to say. He said something to this effect, "Warren, this desire of yours to go to college is good. Your studies and experiences will take you much further along the path of life than I have chosen. You'll do fine. Remember you can make a living with your hands, but using both your hands and your mind will be the best combination."

He waited for a response. All I could do was nod. I found myself wanting to put on a pair of gloves and start pulling nails, helping him as I had always done. Guilty feelings took over. In a few minutes, I would drive off into an unknown future, leaving him alone, working so very hard. He stood up and said he had a gift. He walked to his truck and from the front seat, picked up something, brought it over, and sat down. He handed me a book. It was reddish with gold letters. *Think and Grow Rich* by Napoleon Hill (Figure 13). I said, "Thank you." I knew the value of books and recall him saying something like, "Warren I believe in you and what you are about to start, your life's journey. Now, I want you to study this book, learn the secrets and apply them. If you are the young man that I know, you will do as I have requested. You will accomplish wonderful things and have a great life. It will take lots of work and a mountain of mistakes, but you will succeed." He smiled and his eyes teared.

Dad screwed the plastic cup back on the thermos and set it on the metal tool box. "Warren, you best be going if you want to reach Lubbock before nightfall." We stood up. Under his breath, he said, "I love you son," and pulled me into his big chest with a bear hug. I turned around and slowly walked to the car. Opening the door, I turned and extended a hand. He returned a slight wave. A lonely sigh escaped from my lungs, as I started the car and turned onto the street. The window was rolled down. My shirt sleeve caught the wind. Not interested in the radio, I listened to the tires making sizzling sounds on the hot pavement. I drove without thoughts for hours, I was gone.

Figure 13:Dad's gift, Napoleon Hill's book "Think and Grow Rich"

"This book contains the secret, after having been put to a practical test by thousands of people, in almost every walk of life."
Mr. Hill

◈ CHAPTER FOUR ◈

End Of My Rope

"If you want answers ask many friends and select only the best results."
Dad

Fall semester, I could have been the poster boy for the "green" freshman kid. The first day, I got lost looking for the registrar's office at Texas Tech, Lubbock, Texas and wound up at their agricultural farms. Eventually, I did find the registrar's office and enrolled in the school of architectural engineering, the design option. The day I left home, driving an old 49 Chrysler packed with everything I owned, (which was very little) I was debt free with $350 in cash. My parents helped pave the way for a job washing dishes for Harold and Francis Medlock, owners of the Top of the Plains Restaurant. The restaurant was on the top floor of the tallest building for a hundred miles in any direction. The twentieth-floor view of West Texas is best described as flat as a ruler. I slept in my car for three nights in the parking lot of an all-night truck stop. Asking questions about a place to live, I followed a lead out of Lubbock to Slaton, 16 miles away. A job cleaning earned me a room in the back storage behind a beauty shop in a residential neighborhood (Figure 14). The accommodation was a kitchen used for the storage of beauty supplies and used furniture. The room was sealed off from the front part of the house with a 4'x8' sheet of raw plywood. The bathroom was inside the beauty shop. This meant I had to go outside by a side door around to the front to use the shower and toilet shared by the customers.

Figure 14: Beauty Shop in Slaton, Texas

I learned to wash dishes in the devil's hot water and was compensated with a late afternoon snack, supper and seventy-five cents an hour. My schedule was to attend early morning classes, architectural labs in the afternoon and drive downtown at four to wash unending stacks of dishes. At eight pm, I drove sixteen miles to Slaton, Texas, to wash towels and push a broom at a beauty shop. I finished about ten.

Once a month on Saturday, I had a stinky, greasy job; a trip to the restaurant's roof to clean the grease trap.

The metal box that collected cooking grease from vents in the kitchen needed to be scraped clean. It was not as bad as pulling nails in the city dump. Remembering that smelly job made this work tolerable. Happy to be finished, I drove back to Slaton to my room behind the beauty shop.

The worn key opened an old lock that must have had a million turnings during its lifetime. I felt "moved in" after a week. The warm, somewhat stale room, was as I had left it. The bed, with an old faded quilt, felt good to stretch out on. It was clean and soft, with batting that poked through like the frayed seats in Dad's old truck. I looked at the ceiling. The once brightly colored wallpaper had small groups of flowers that were turning the color of old ivory. The flowers were marked by concentric circles of lacy brown water stains. Years of rainwater had trickled its way from the asphalt shingle roof, adding yet another splotchy layer to the paper ceiling. An ancient oriental carpet with half a dozen worn spots covered the bumpy wooden floor. The room had a dresser and a vanity. When opened, the dark wood dresser gave off a distinct aroma of "old".

I opened the door to add fresh air to the space I had created. On Saturday afternoons, the beauty shop was a bee hive of women. Almost every high-pitched word spoken on the other side of the plywood wall was audible. I put on one of the seven piano concerto records to escape the noisy hair dryers and gossipy chatter. I dozed off for a few brief minutes. I woke to the sound of the needle scratching around and around.

I had been thinking about Dad and the book he had given me. I decided to read a few pages. Opening the book for the first time, I discovered Dad had written a few lines on the first page. I smiled as I read.

Warren,
I have dated this book March 26th,
1960, not the date I gave you this gift,
but the date I told you that your
Mother and I loved you and you
would always be welcomed here. I broke
your plate. Breaking your plate was a
rough day for me, knowing you needed
your wings and it was time. I love
you and Charles so very much, both
very different, but both good young
men. Keep your faith for it will hold
you together more than anything
else in this world. Live life with courage
and conviction and always be true to
yourself. I am proud of the man you
have become.
Respectfully, your father,
Loren Taft Cullar

I had a lump in my throat the size of a baseball. All I could do was stare out into the driveway. I took a deep breath, stood up, went into the kitchen and poured a big glass of water to wash down the lump. Walking out onto the small concrete porch, I remembered Dad and his brief farewell talk. He really hadn't finished his thoughts in the broom factory that day; not until this moment. Sitting on the cement steps, I placed the glass down and opened the book. I was curious about this book and why it was so special to Dad. I read the chapter's introduction and the table of contents to familiarize myself with the writing. The book was full of quotes, interviews and self-examination. I was impressed by the fact the author had spent 20 years in research. With a letter from Andrew Carnegie, he interviewed 500 of the wealthiest people, inquiring as to how they accumulated their wealth. At the time, at 5'-2" tall, Andrew Carnegie was the world's wealthiest man. I returned to the drafting table. Sunlight was coming through the slatted wooden blinds, making stripes across the Texas flag I had thumb tacked to the east wall. I continued reading without realizing my journey had begun.

Freshman first semester was measured in repetitious hours of work, study and classes. (i.e. wash, rinse, dry and repeat.) If I were to add all those hours for a day, each day would total more than 25 hours. During this period things started to slip. My grades were going over a cliff. Often, I was too tired to study after cleaning the shop. Life in my hamster wheel was going faster and faster. Weekends were full of things to do; washing clothes, study and architectural projects, odd jobs and church. I was barely managing. After months of the same thing over and over, I became lonely and discouraged. I had no friends, no time off, only a tight schedule of work and more work. One night after cleaning the shop, I locked up and trudged through the snow to the side porch and room. The cold was penetrating, I sat on the edge of the bed. Tears and sobs seeped out of me. There was nothing left except exhaustion. I pulled the covers back, kicked off the shoes and crawled in without taking off my clothes. The next morning, I managed to get to class, but in a daze of mental anguish I wasn't keeping up. At the restaurant, I robotically washed dishes for hours. Harold, the owner and cook, left the kitchen to sit at the counter and have a glass of warm milk. This was his normal routine after closing. I finished the dishes and cleaned the grill. I propped my elbows up on the edge of the sink to watch the water drain. I kept watching until the last drop disappeared. Inside I was screaming. I mumbled, "I can't take this anymore." My vision blurred. My head hurt. I mumbled again, "I can't do this anymore." Quickly, I reached under the sink and pulled out a small crate. Without thinking, I stepped onto the edge of the sink and opened the large sliding window. I stared into the blackness, mesmerized by the shimmering street lights twenty stories below. A light snow was falling. The street noise was muffled.

I was in a dream experience. I imagined myself on the top diving board of an Olympic size pool. I was dressed in Marine Corps combat gear including a pack and an old water-soaked M1rifle. The drill instructor yelled, "Recruit, keep your eyes straight ahead and step off." It was easy, to take one step to free fall. Suddenly a rush of cold air from the outside, jarred me into the present. I was staring twenty stories below into nothingness. Those thoughts of free falling felt real, where did they come from?

The kitchen door banged open and Harold walked in, still reading his evening paper. I turned, pulled a rag out of my apron and pretended I was cleaning the vent hood. My mind thought, "Was I going to step out?" I frowned. My hands were shaking.

Harold asked, "Warren, are you all right, what's wrong?" I managed a weak reply that I was tired and needed some sleep. I tossed the apron in the cleaning basket, grabbed my coat off the back of the kitchen door and walked down the hall to the elevator. I pushed the down button. I could have died a few moments ago. I felt stupid and scared.

In the snowy alley, a street lamp created a triangular cone of lighted snowflakes above my car. The night was soft and silent. I fumbled with the keys and discovered that the car was unlocked. I opened the back door. All my drafting equipment had been stolen. I sat down in the backseat and stared blankly at the snow-covered windshield. I felt victimized. At least the thief had missed the drafting set lying on the floor.

I drove home on a dark winter road in the blowing snow. I felt violated and stupid for not locking the car. I had no extra time or money. When I arrived, college tuition cost $50, books and gas. A few added things for school quickly depleted my $350 of seed money. Weekly pay was a few dollars. A pack of Juicy Fruit gum was a luxury. During the drive home, I beat myself up pretty-good. I yelled, "I want to change! I want a better place to live and a job that pays more money." I was not going to let a thief or anything stop me, not even myself, from earning a college degree. I wanted to improve everything, but I didn't know how. I was angry but also strong. I knew that I would find an answer, I would win.

Back at the room, I pushed open the screen door which had collected a drift of snow at the threshold. The room was as cold as the inside of a refrigerator. I turned up the gas stove, pulled on long underwear, two pairs of socks and piled on a second blanket. I lay awake for a long time, watching the shadows from the gas stove dance on the ceiling. My breath was like vanishing fog in the freezing room. It was still cold under the covers.

I wanted better; something better. I wanted to live in a warm place and have a job that paid more money.

While getting warm, I reflected on Dad's words from our broom factory conversation. Dad reminded me, **"Son, your decision and desire to go to college is a good direction and working with your hands is good, but working with your hands and your mind is better."** Truth! I was only washing dishes and cleaning a beauty shop.

"The starting point of all achievements is desire and the influence of that desire on your entire thinking can motivate one to move or change the present moment into something new and exciting."

Mr. Hill

◈ CHAPTER FIVE ◈

READ *THINK AND GROW RICH*

"Son, what you think about, you become."
Dad

Even through the plywood, the cackling of beauty operators startled me out of a deep sleep. "Hell, it's nine o'clock! I've missed classes and half the day!" I got up, pulled on my bathrobe, and rolled up the vellum-colored door shade. Six inches of a late winter snow had turned my car into a giant marshmallow. Dressed only in a bathrobe, I did a tip toe dance through wet snow to the bathroom. I smiled, as several ladies under the hair dryers dropped their jaws. I went back to the room and heated a pot of water while ripping open a box of tea bags. I glared at the bright white landscape. Hot tea and a day-old donut was breakfast.

Life was a maze of washing dishes and pushing a broom along with a full load of college classes. I hardly had time to attend, much less study. I was a lab rat scurrying to find his way to the cheese, but there was no cheese. The book from Dad had something about a burning desire. Hill's book was on the board book shelf next to the drafting table. I sipped tea as I flipped through the contents of Think and Grow Rich, chapter two, "Burning Desire" and chapter three, "Faith." I read the first chapters several times, to make sure I grasped what Hill was writing. I breathed heavily, my forehead creased and my teeth clenched, not in anger, but in determination. I did have a burning desire to accomplish something better for myself. All thoughts began taking on Hill's description of burning desire. I had a burning desire to change. I reached across the desk and tore out a single sheet of notebook paper, took a deep breath and scribbled the following:

I WILL FIND A NEW PLACE TO LIVE
AND MAKE MORE MONEY
I WILL FIND A NEW PLACE TO LIVE
AND MAKE MORE MONEY
I WILL FIND A NEW PLACE TO LIVE
AND MAKE MORE....

I forced the ball point pen, cutting into the paper. I continued writing the statement dozens of times using both sides of the paper. With each repetition, I strengthened the confidence to make the decision a reality. I thumb-tacked the page to the center of the Texas Flag on the wall (Figure 15). I looked at the note. I had fashioned a definite plan right out of Hill's book. It was not exact, but it would suffice.

Spring break, I was looking forward to seeing the folks and not-so-little brother. After work on Friday, I drove out of Slaton. The windshield caught a few droplets of a late afternoon shower. The big, blue Chrysler hugged the road at 55 mph. Arriving late, I parked and went in by way of the den. I stood in shock. My painting of the western mesas and winding river had disappeared into a sea foam green stucco wall. Mother had painted over my proudest artwork. I was furious. The mural was gone. Glaring at the wall of new paint, I realized that my dream, my aspirations didn't mean a thing to her.

Figure 15: Texas flag with note tacked to the wall

Mom was three when her Mother died of Tuberculosis. Her Papa Pohl burned the bedding and gave Annie, the baby, to his twin sister. He put the other three young children in a covered wagon and spent three months working and traveling to Lubbock, Texas from Victoria, Texas. Mother grew up in a sheet iron shack on the outskirts of Lubbock with her Papa and her two brothers. I do not know the circumstances of why she went to live with another couple when she was 12 or 13. Mrs. Williams was an overbearing woman and a clean freak. Mother was required to clean everything. She grew up in a real Cinderella existence, only there were no step sisters and no

Cinderella ending. The habit of cleaning stuck with her, but not to the point of fanaticism. Mother became tough and a bit stubborn because she had to survive. The tension between us had always been there. I bristled when I entered the kitchen and gave her a dutiful kiss on the cheek. Nothing was ever said about the wall painting.

Dad yelled from the back porch, "That you Warren?" "Yes Sir!" Dad was reading. He stood up. We exchanged big bear hugs and sat down for a long talk. I don't know who was more excited to see the other. Dad said, "You're doing well. I knew you were man enough to be on your own." His support meant a lot. We talked about the architectural studies, cleaning the beauty shop and washing dishes for Harold Medlock. I spoke about the long hours and how I had reached the end of my rope. I didn't tell him how close I had come to stepping out of the restaurant window to my death. Not locking the car and the theft of my drafting supplies was not mentioned either. I did not want to explain and embarrass myself. I shared reading Hill's book and writing a burning desire statement, now thumb tacked to the center of the Texas flag. He applauded the actions.

Brother Charles joined us on the porch. He talked about his job at the air conditioner supply company and showed off his newest "junker" car he was overhauling in the driveway. We laughed about my lack of mechanical ability and how good I was at holding the light while he worked. Uncles, cousins, every man in the family could work on anything mechanical. To me, anything with bolts and wires was boring. I preferred to draw. I had two days filled with home cooked chicken-fried steak and visiting family and friends. The weekend was over too soon. Sunday morning, we had an early breakfast, attended service at the Vine

Street Church of Christ, then lunch at McEplines' cafeteria.

I drove back to the flattest land in Texas into the season's first sand storm. The vast Texas plains had long been stripped of buffalo grass, plowed under and replaced by deep furrows of irrigated cotton. The fields, as far as the eye can see, are bare in early spring. Winds blow up clouds of dirt turning them into sand storms. You can feel the sand in your teeth and hear it blasting the paint off your car as you drive. One sand colored day in April, I heard about an assistant job at the El Lora Motel, owned by a Mrs. Wicker. It was only a few blocks from the beauty shop. I called and asked for a time to meet her and talk about the position. The one story red brick motel had 16 rooms in the center of town, catching almost every traveler at the traffic light (Figure 16).

Figure 16: El Lora Motel, Slaton, Texas

Mrs. Wicker was a thin woman, about 60. Her dark hair with wisps of white was gathered in a tight bun. Glasses dangled from a gold chain against a dark flower print dress. Her long thin fingers held a cigarette with an inch-long ash, poised to fall, yet never did. We talked. She needed assistance at the motel because her long-time employee had moved away to be with her family.

Mrs. Wicker was serious, polite and reserved. I'm sure she saw me as a young kid finding his way in the world. After an hour of casual conversation, she outlined the requirements. I would check in guests after 11 pm, run errands for Mrs. Wicker and the guests, and do small jobs around the motel. She offered to pay me $20 a week. Her maid, Maria, would clean my room. Mrs. Wicker would prepare our evening meal. I was free to go out until 11:00 on nights when she played bridge in the reception room. She invited me on a tour of the motel and escorted me into the kitchen. She opened the door on the right. "Warren, would you like to work here, and do you think you would be comfortable in this room?"

My first impression was soft carpet, warm colored drapes, (not roll down paper shades,) and a full-size bed. There was a cushy wing backed arm chair with a floor lamp perfect for reading and enough room for the drafting table and stool. I quickly answered, "YES," as I smiled from ear to ear. NOW, I was a big believer in the power of Hill's book about burning desire. I put faith and desire into action, had written my affirmation and was reaping the rewards. I would repeat this burning desire "goal setting" process throughout life.

I turned the key to my dingy old room. I yanked the thumbtacks out of the note and yelled at the top of my lungs the words, "I will find a new place to live and make more money!" I had a new job, a better place to live and more money exactly as I had written. The Texas flag was folded into a correct military triangle, a symbolic act that

I was leaving the kid behind. Never again would I allow myself to be caught in that kind of negative situation. Achieving the goal was a grand experience. I announced I had a better offer and was taking it without a two-week notice. "Thank you" for the room. I moved fast. By late afternoon I was packed, moved and settled into the new space at the motel. The bedroom had a carpeted bathroom. I had never seen anything like that before.

Mrs. Wicker and I became acquainted in conversation over dinner. Although the food was good and filling, I was more appreciative than hungry. Since it wasn't a bridge night, we spent the evening reviewing the procedures for checking in guests, where to purchase cigarettes and any other items the guests might need. After we finished, I walked around to the back of the motel. I went down the alley for another couple of blocks. I looked down the empty street where I had lived for many months. It seemed like a life time ago. Self-confidence was improving by the minute. I had a grand comfortable place to live, a much-improved salary and Mrs. Wicker was pleasant.

She retired to her bedroom and I stayed up watching the late-night news for the first time in months, getting familiar with the new surroundings. I did a "walk about", maybe it was a celebration dance. The large reception/living room was decorated with exquisite antique furniture and satin-like green drapes. In the bedroom, I finished unpacking and slid into the soft wing backed chair. I grinned, surveying the room. The drafting table was ready and my clothes were hung neatly in a real closet with a door. For once my books were on a small table, not on boards separated by bricks. The bedside floor lamp was spot-on for reading. Opening Hill's book, I retraced the first part of the book and marveled at how it was working that very moment. I drifted off, warm and content.

The office door bell chimed at 12:32 am I bolted out of the chair. I registered my first guest, turned on the "No Vacancy" sign and went to bed. With a new job and a great living situation, my focus was on the remaining classes, with more time to study. The hours of washing dishes were cut and didn't seem so overwhelming. I smiled much more. Life was becoming exciting. I spent bridge night, Friday evenings, sitting on a quilt-covered porch swing with a sweet, sixteen-year-old dark eyed brunette talking about my architectural studies and her high school activities.

I had hit bottom and picked myself up, discovering I had not been in control. I re-committed to earning a college degree and wrote the first goal to find a better place to live and make more money. That goal had been accomplished in a short time. I became a true believer in the secrets found in the book. I proved it then and have been proving it for fifty years. I am prosperous because of goal setting. Faith in yourself is the ability to get up one more time and start over. When you find yourself in a position where the status quo is intolerable, draw your line in the sand. Find the faith to step over that line and seize a better life.

"Faith is the visualization of and belief in the attainment of Desire. Only those who become money conscious ever accumulate great riches. If you do not see great riches in your imagination, you will never see them in your bank balance. A burning desire is the starting point of all achievement. The method, by which desire for riches can be transmuted into its financial equivalent, consists of six definite, practical steps.

1. Fix in your mind the exact amount of money you desire.

2. What will you give in exchange for the money?

3. Establish a date when you intend to possess the money.

4. Create a plan for carrying out your desires.

5. Write out a clear statement, amount, date and what you will exchange.

6. Read your statement morning and night."

Mr. Hill

CHAPTER SIX

Joined the Marines & Back in College

"Son, either fish or cut bait."
Dad

The Vietnam War was escalating, and the draft was calling up young men. Sometime in the spring I would probably be drafted. I walked to the North end of Texas Tech campus to the Marine Corps Station and talked to the Marine recruiter. I told him I really wanted to continue going to college and I didn't want to get drafted. He suggested that I join the Marine Reserves. I would go to boot camp for three months and combat training for an additional three months. At the end of training, when duty assignments were issued, my orders would be as a 7-year reservist, assigned to the closest unit where I lived. I felt confident that I would become a Marine. The first day of spring, March 21st, 1962 was a major decision day. Standing at attention and raising my right hand, I took an oath.

"I, Warren Cullar, do solemnly swear that I will obey the orders of the President of the United States and the orders of the officers appointed over me, according to the regulations and the uniform code of military justice. So, help me God."

With this oath, I joined the United States Marine Corps.

I called Mother and told her I had signed up. A good guess is that she realized I was grown and she had to look at our relationship through different glasses.

The waiting room of the bus station in Lubbock was crowded. I went to the door, watching for my tall skinny brother. Even though we grew up together, I can't remember him clearly. When we were younger, I thought of Charles as the enemy because we always got into fights. When caught, Mother would make us go cut our switches off the "switch bush" next to the corner of the garage.

Charles, now taller than me but still my "little" brother, ambled off the bus, looked around and waved when he saw me. He said, "Let's eat." We found a favorite burger place and he ordered half the menu. I said, "Charles, you're eating like a horse." He laughed. I was glad to see him and realized he had put some meat on his bones.

Normally he didn't have much to say but occasionally he could out talk me. Today was one of those days. He was working part time and had registered for college classes. He never finished high school and as he tells the story himself, "If you look up the word procrastinator in the dictionary you will see my picture."

He had taken the bus so he could drive me to the airport the next day. He would use the car until I returned from six months of training. It would be my second plane flight. The first flight was as a cub scout with the scout pack. That flight took only thirty minutes on a military transport. I remember the deafening noise from the huge propeller engines. Now, I was flying on a jet to the Marine training base in San Diego, California. I found a seat, sat down and relaxed my grip on the envelope that contained the orders from the Marine Corps. I was nervous, not about flying, but about going to boot camp.

I knew it was going to be tough though I was in good physical shape. I had the confidence to become a Marine. The sergeant told me what to expect the first days of boot camp. What he said and what happened was a major glitch in communication. Yes, they were going to cut my hair, but I didn't know I would be standing in lines all the time. When my turn came, a gorilla sized marine grabbed me by the collar and slammed me into a barber chair. The marine drill instructors yelled orders over the roar of electric clippers. Eight barbers were cutting hair simultaneously and each trim took about 35 seconds. I was back in line crammed into the man in front of me, my nose almost touching the guys neck. I could see blood trickling down the back of his head. I was pushed forward, but there was no place to go. I had seen sheep sheared more humanely.

The drill instructors (D.I.s) yelled at us! The meanest looking drill sergeant had a flattened, hard, angular shaped face with a reddish crew cut and beady eyes. His shirt was perfectly pressed and his boots so highly polished, they would reflect, as he said later, "The color of your girlfriend's panties." He yelled, "Run outside and stand at attention on the yellow footprints painted on the asphalt." There were 150 foot prints. I stood still; I knew enough to not lock my knees to prevent collapsing. I thought of that after an hour had passed and my legs were cramping. We were not going anywhere until there was a man on each set of footprints. We waited on buses, trains, airplanes and drop offs, all to deliver the next would be marines. Scalped young men ran to find a set of foot prints, slowly filling in what would be our 75-man platoon. My leg muscles flinched. I moved to ease the pain. Somewhere in the background another D.I. yelled at me. What was he calling me? A maggot? Yes, it was Maggot!

We were marched everywhere; first to get measured for our uniforms and then to take a shower. We changed into our boots, trousers, cap and bright yellow sweat shirt with the Marine Corps emblem in red. Our platoon of shaved headed recruits all looked the same except for size and color.

The first night we were billeted in temporary barracks and required to put all our new clothes into a sea bag, then into temporary lockers. A wise ass kid with an attitude said something I didn't hear. The D.I. crammed him into a wall locker simultaneously kicking the hell out of him. He then slammed the door and spent more minutes cussing and kicking the metal door. We all stood at attention. I had a clear view of the scene. I thought I was going to piss my pants. The D.I. just kept kicking the guy. My body was shaking, wishing I hadn't joined. The D.I. yelled, "Anyone else got a smart mouth?" Several of us mumbled "no sir." "You Pussies, I can't hear you, now does anyone else have a SMART MOUTH?" A chorus of "NO SIR" raised the roof. Another D.I. pulled the guy out of the locker. His nose was squirting blood. We never saw the guy again. I was frightened.

Sleep was difficult because men kept arriving and the lights were always on. The next morning, wearing our yellow sweat shirts, we marched or waddled like a big yellow blob to the chow hall; then another long day of standing in lines. We went through the medical exams in our birthday suits. Every inch of the body was examined. We were fingerprinted, photographed and received the first of dozens of shots in each arm at the same time with air guns. The guns caused a quarter size swelling to appear in an instant. A six-foot recruit in front of me took his turn for shots and he deflated like a balloon. One of the D.I.'s made that guy suffer for passing out.

The most civil D.I. was more human than the other Neanderthals, but that did not keep him from being tough. My first encounter with Sergeant Sullivan was when he was going over the paper work and asked my serial number. I said, "I don't know it." He replied, "Wrong Answer!" I learned to say quickly, "1945814 Sir." I caught on that everything started and ended with "Sir." Next, he yelled, "Cullar you're too damn short by half an inch to be a Marine!" I yelled back, "Sir, I will grow!" His response, "Cullar you're in the Marines! Next!"

The platoon of 75 by graduation had been reduced by a dozen; the man in front of me broke his finger and was sent back. The guy behind me couldn't take it and went over the fence or AWOL (absent without leave). I gained 28 pounds of muscle and the belief that I could do anything.

The morning finally came, graduation. The Marine Corps transformed me physically and mentally (Figure 17). Our platoon marched in perfect cadence. Shoes were polished to a reflective shine. Our uniforms were

Figure 17: Pvt Warren Cullar U.S. Marines, 1962

perfectly creased, new muscles filling out the uniform. Mom and Dad had driven from Texas to attend the ceremonies. When the music, speeches and parade were over we were dismissed to spend lunch with our families.

My parents made the same drive three years later to see Charles graduate. Our parents were proud to have two sons as Marines. After graduation from boot camp we moved from San Diego MCRD to Camp Pendleton, California for three months of combat training.

We spent three weeks at the rifle range learning how to fire our weapons. I learned how to kill with a variety of weapons and became a bad ass. It gave me the confidence that I could go into combat to defend our country. The decision to be a Marine is not for everyone, but for that time and place in life, the discipline and training were exactly what I needed. I was breaking my own plate now. Becoming a Marine was one of the best and most powerful decisions I ever made.

Sergeant Sullivan smiled as he handed me a large envelope with my name, rank and serial number printed in the center. He said, "Cullar, you've become a good Marine. Good luck." He gripped my hand with strength. This was different from the first day when he yelled at me for not knowing my serial number and called me Maggot. The orders were to report to the Marine training station on the Tech campus and be in the reserves for the next seven years. I didn't have to go to Viet Nam. I have two friends who did and their names are on The Wall in Washington D.C. honoring those who gave their lives in Viet Nam. "Semper Fi".

I returned to Texas where I found a job painting houses for the next several months. Spring semester I returned to Tech and shared an apartment with Douglas Johnson (Duck). Duck was an acquaintance from high school. He was small in stature, had narrow features, high cheekbones and was losing his hair at the age of 23. He had an air that projected success. He worked with his father, sold real estate and was somewhat successful. I bought my first investment from him; five acres of raw land south of Abilene, Texas for thirty dollars a month including interest. He aspired to become a mortgage broker. He dressed like one and acted the part. At the Episcopal Resale Shop, Duck taught me how to dress. I purchased some nice second-hand clothes for a few bucks, including a red and black silk trimmed smoking jacket and a suit. I looked sharp and felt successful in that dark blue suit.

In the student union, I met "Blue Eyes", a pretty student with dark hair. I got laid at age 23. At first sex was awkward, but I caught on very quickly. We dated that Spring semester. The door knob to the apartment often had a tie hanging on it. Thankfully, Duck spent an inordinate amount of time in the library that semester.

I walked a mile across campus on the way to our apartment. The November air was biting at my nose and ears. I stepped into a bookstore to get warm. A book spoke to me. I pulled it off the shelf, read the title on the spine and bought it. The book store, a block off Broadway, was on the way back to the two story white castle apartments. Most of the students knew the vintage apartment house. Many students had lived there from the early thirties to the present. Ten minutes later I was listening to familiar squeaks as I climbed the staircase to the second floor. Keys rattled. I opened the door and was hit with delicious smells of chicken and garlic. Duck was cooking. He cooked. I cleaned. We both did an excellent job. I exclaimed, "Sorry boss, the lab work in the greenhouse took longer than expected." Duck said, "Put the plates out, we're eating."

The next afternoon was geology lab. At the door, I picked up a box of rocks to identify and headed to the back row. A crashing sound from the front of the room caused the entire class to jump. The professor had thrown a boulder onto his desk. He yelled, "That was a boulder, do you know the definition of a boulder?" He wanted our attention and he got it. ("Boulder: 1. a smooth rounded mass of rock that has a diameter greater than 25 cm and that has been shaped by erosion and transported by ice or water from its original position." (Collins English Dictionary))

The class was Geology G102, a basic elective. By the fifth year of college my grades were showing "A" results. After identifying all 24 specimens in about twenty minutes, an hour ahead of schedule, I pulled out the new book from a weathered leather brief case. I read the title: *How to Make a Living as a Painter* by Kenneth Harris. I had thought of owning an art gallery to sell my work; a gallery that also included the works of other freelance artists as well. Truth... I had never set foot in a gallery. I came up with a business name: "Gallery House of Cullar" (rather pompous sounding). I designed a business card and a gallery sign on the inside cover of the book. When class ended, I turned in the tray of rocks. I finished the semester at Texas Tech.

"Those who reach DECISIONS promptly and definitely know what they want, and generally get it."

Mr. Hill

CHAPTER SEVEN

First Gallery & Embezzlement

"Plan your work, work your plan."
Dad

I discovered I could graduate from Abilene Christian College in one year rather than almost two years from Texas Tech. I was ready to finish. I was invited to stay in Dad's rent house behind his business and finish the last year of college in Abilene. The previous semester at Tech, I had taken courses in freehand drawing, perspective, two and three-dimensional design and an architectural watercolor painting class. I enjoyed the course work in those classes to the point of changing majors to finish with a degree in fine art. The idea of owning a gallery also came from the success in those classes. I decided to take the initiative to turn the dream of ownership into a reality. I stayed up late writing and planning a gallery. I devised a plan to sell Dad on the idea of using his rent house as a gallery and living space. I would remodel the apartment into Abilene's first art gallery. The entire plan was in place. I collected information about operating a gallery business, but I still had never been in an art gallery. I was following a burning desire to be an entrepreneur. Dad said, "I will help you create your business." I was excited about his offer and his help. The rental property would be rent free for one year, his way of assisting with the plan. Two of the rooms were designed as gallery space. The third room was a multipurpose kitchen, office and bedroom.

For most of Dad's working life he did not follow the simple rule of "Plan your work, work your plan" and as a result he failed often. When I started working with him at age 12, he had accumulated enough lessons from the school of hard knocks to settle into the working and planning stage of his life.

I printed business cards and met with artists who wanted to be represented in the gallery. The Gallery House of Cullar was beginning to take shape (Figure 18). Mrs. Henigan, the high school art teacher, was a great source of inspiration. Twelve artists joined the adventure in opening the gallery. They paid a small monthly fee, plus a percentage, when their art sold.

Figure 18: First Gallery Sign, 1965

Two weeks before the opening, I got a call from "Blue Eyes" in Lubbock. She wanted to see me. She had graduated, found a job with a Lubbock bank and moved to the Tumble Weed Trailer Court. Two days later, I walked up the three steps to her trailer and knocked on the door. I could hear Cole Porter music. She opened the door, smoking a filtered cigarette. She gave me a French Kiss. It was like licking the inside of an ash tray, "Yuck!" I didn't like the smell of her smoke and our conversation was tense. Crushing her cigarette out in a Mickey Mouse ash tray, she offered me a glass of Jack Daniels. I said, "Make it a splash only."

I was glad to see her. She was very attractive with those beautiful blue eyes and she looked sexy in her tight sweater. We went out to dinner and finished the evening with great sex. She brought up the idea of getting married, as she had done this once before. I wasn't in love then and I still wasn't in love. Marriage was not what I wanted. I stated unequivocally, "NO, I DON'T WANT TO GET MARRIED!" She yelled, "Well, I'm pregnant and if you don't marry me, I will have an abortion. Now do you want to marry me?" I stood up and nervously said, "I am not ready to get married, NO, I Don't Want to Marry You."

She was crying and yelling at the same time, "Then you pay the $750 dollars for an abortion, if you don't pay me I'll tell your Dad." I folded on that blackmail statement. She knew how close I was to Dad. He would never get over that news, it would destroy our relationship. I was shaking and yelling, "I'll send you $200 when I get back to Abilene and the rest later." She snarled, "It better be damn soon." She opened the trailer door. I stepped out. She slammed the door. The trailer shook. I stood looking at the door wondering what had happened?

I drove back to Abilene. It was about two in the morning when I pulled into an all-night truck stop for coffee. I was worried. Sleep was not an option. There was about $200 dollars in a checking account, but I had no other way to get the remainder of the blackmail money. I was more worried about Dad finding out than about getting the money. Thinking aloud, I said, "I didn't want to get married. I don't want to get married."

The night felt darker than usual. My hands were on the steering wheel, but my thoughts were somewhere else. Specks of light on the horizon soon burst into bright headlights that flashed by. Moments later the pavement disappeared into weeds. In the same instant, I yelled, "HELL, NO!" and slammed on the brakes. The car pulled hard to the right, scraping gravel, raced down a steep slope, then jerked to a stop. The bumper had caught a small tree and snapped it off. Dust engulfed the car and the headlights disappeared into a cloud of dirt. Heart pounding, I turned off the engine. The dust boiled up then settled into the headlight beams. I was not injured, but my adrenaline was working overtime. I was in shock and couldn't focus. I yelled in confusion, "What happened?"

My fuzzy head thought, who was I talking to? With folded arms, I buried my face on the steering wheel and turned off the headlights. I was exhausted. Some time passed. I jumped when a flashlight beam filled the dark interior of the car. I heard banging on the window. A white-haired man yelled, "Are you all right?" I rolled down the window and told him, "I'm okay, must have fallen asleep." I opened the door and scrambled out and up the slope. He said, "You'll need some help getting out of that ditch. I've got some chains in the back of the pickup." I thanked the fellow.

In a few minutes I was once more on the way to Abilene. I noticed the early sun breaking through the clouds above the mesquite trees. I thought, "That was one hell of a night."

A day after I got back from Lubbock, Blue Eyes called, "Warren, damn you! Send me the money now!" I had no other choice. I fearfully pulled out the big check book from the bottom desk drawer. The title "West Texas Art Club" was printed on the cover. Three months earlier I had been appointed to the treasurer position. Upset, scared and nervous, I wrote a check for cash, $550 to send to Blue Eyes. The amount was almost the entire account. I was now committing a crime. I was embezzling the club's money. If caught, jail would be in my future. Religious beliefs were being destroyed. Everything I was doing was wrong.

I mailed the money to Blue Eyes, then I worked extra jobs and sold several of my watercolors to scrape together the stolen funds before the next treasurer took over. The club's books balanced. No one was the wiser, except me. That year, I grew old because of all the anxious times. Alka-Seltzer was the cocktail of the evening. I was so naïve, I didn't think about asking Blue Eyes to show me proof she was pregnant. Years later, my friend Duck found out from her that she was never pregnant. She only wanted to get even for not marrying her.

At the gallery, we were ready for the big opening September 11, 1965. The Gallery House of Cullar celebrated with twelve artists, my former art teacher plus an enthusiastic crowd of well-wishers. Several paintings sold. After nine long months, art sales were not making enough money for me to live on. I gave up. All the advertising, word of mouth, even the display at the First State Bank, did nothing to encourage people to walk down a short alley to buy art. Having learned a lot, I gave myself a grade of "A" in business 101, but an "F" in location. I learned that I never wanted to run an art gallery in the future. I failed fast and made new plans to get up and start over again. The gallery sign in the tiny yard was pulled up. The box of letterheads was ceremoniously dumped into the alley trash can and the gallery was turned back into Dad's rent house.

I graduated from college and found a part time job as an instructor teaching watercolor lessons at the YWCA in a "broom closet" to eight ladies. The room was small. There were two card tables for the students to paint on. To save space I put a one gallon can of water in the center of each table. The students were seated, I entered, a little nervous and accidentally kicked the table leg. Both gallons of water spilled into the students' laps. After that start, teaching watercolor was easy and a thoroughly enjoyable experience.

"When temporary defeat comes accept the fact that your plans are not sound, just rebuid."
Mr. Hill

◈ CHAPTER EIGHT ◈

Wrong Wife & First Jobs

"A quitter never wins and a winner never quits."
Dad

I met Audrey at the gallery the second or third week after the opening. She was overweight, wore no make-up and her hair was in pig tails. She told me she liked to do craft work, like macramé and batik. She explained the process of dying fabric by using hot wax to save the color from each dye job. Multi layers of dye and waxing produce beautiful shades of many colors and designs. The next time I saw Audrey was eight months later. She came with her parents to my senior art exhibit at the college. Her Mother had been my 7th grade math teacher and our families belonged to the same church. Audrey looked attractive, she had lost weight, was wearing make-up and her hair was styled. She made it obvious that she was interested in me. We started dating. We enjoyed hiking and looking for flint arrowheads. We became members of the local Archaeological Society. I liked being with her because she was smart, had an adventurous spirit and did a variety of creative craft work. She was also opinionated and criticized anything that didn't please her. The critic in her became obvious later.

My family was on a weekend trip to visit relatives in West Texas, I was driving Dad's big Chrysler. Audrey, Charles and his girlfriend Grace were all in the large front seat. The folks sat in the back. It was raining lightly, I slowed down on a curve coming into Post, Texas. A thin layer of water covered the highway. I braked. I braked again with all my strength. I shrieked, "We're going to hit! Tires won't hold!" at 30 mph. Chrome bumpers slammed together. CRASH! In slow motion, the white hood of our car buckled up like a folding sheet of aluminum foil in your hand. Screams! Tearing metal! Bodies slammed into the dashboard, windows and each other. There was an abrupt stop. My vision blurred. I lost consciousness. When my brain regained function, I heard blaring sirens. Someone was trying to help me out of the car. A cold rain soaked us as we were loaded into an ambulance. We all went to the hospital. No one was seriously injured, but Audrey was on a gurney and had a hematoma the size of an egg on her forehead. I was scared. I thought she might sue me. I said, "I love you." I was as surprised as she was by these words. I wasn't in love with her. Why did I say that? I have no idea. Maybe I didn't trust her. She held me to that statement. She didn't sue me, but I was sued by the man I crashed into.

A year later, three weeks before our wedding, she cried bitter crocodile tears. She disclosed that her parents had made her give up her illegitimate baby only a few weeks before our first meeting in the gallery. She asked me to forgive her. I did. I was ridiculously naïve in dealing with the opposite sex. Audrey convinced me that our religious views were the same. Our strict religious upbringing was like a shroud over our lives. There was no sex before we were married. On the wedding night when she refused to take the curlers out of her hair, I knew that life was not going to be a fairy tale. Our honeymoon trip was to Saltillo, Mexico. We both felt secure traveling to Mexico and seeking out its history, especially the archaeological sites. On the trip, she disclosed, "Remember my friend Cheryl? She and I planned how I could get you to propose. Cheryl showed me how to improve my appearance and trap you into marrying me." Deceit! Audrey's confession, highlighting her truly nasty nature, would be revisited.

Back home, I sent off several resumes to schools to teach art at the high school level. Nothing came of that effort. I visited a photographer friend who asked me to deliver an envelope of photos to Fidelity Advertising Agency. At the agency, I met their three-commercial artists. I liked them and the professional environment. I inquired about a position. Jody, one of the artists, told me they had no need for an assistant. Leaving the agency, I purchased an expensive black leather portfolio and spent time arranging drawings that showcased my abilities (Figure 19). I called them back for a proper interview and was extended an invitation.

I dressed in a suit, carried the new portfolio and felt professional. All three artists were impressed with the portfolio, not the drawings inside, but the fancy portfolio. Expressing the need to work, I explained, "I will sharpen pencils, take out the trash, anything to assist the agency to produce better results." By a couple weeks later they all had seen a lot of me. One time I dropped by with a dozen donuts. Some folks in the building must have thought I worked at the agency. I'm sure I was hired so I would stop bothering them.

The new job at the agency paid $1.50 an hour, a poor salary, but I was working as a commercial artist and experience was important. One of many jobs was correcting text. The proof readers would send the corrections and I would use an X-ACTO knife to cut out words or letters from proof sheets. I used rubber cement to glue a word or a tiny comma to correct the text. It was tedious work, but I was enjoying the variety of jobs the agency was engaged in, including brochures, annual reports and newspaper layouts. I learned how to use transfers and photographs to create ads.

Figure 19: Example of commercial artwork

During a morning break, I visited with an artist who was hired to build a production set for a photographer. He had recently returned from living in Mexico. He said, "The year, in Mexico was exciting. I learned so much about how to create art and also how to live as an artist." I was intrigued by his stories of studying art at the Instituto de Allende, in San Miguel de Allende, Guanajuato, Mexico. I wrote for information concerning the school and their MFA degree program.

Months passed, I was enjoying the commercial artist position plus a small increase in pay. I was learning from the other three artists and gaining valuable knowledge in advertising. I now contributed to the team. At home my predicament was neither happy nor sad, I was living in a boring relationship. The daily schedule: 1) Make a white bread, peanut butter and strawberry jam sandwich, 2) Add an apple and a bottle of fruit juice, 3) Go to work. Audrey was working as a mobile librarian, checking out a few books at each stop. The remainder of the time she read. It was not a high-pressure job. She wanted to have another baby. I wanted to wait and talk about having a baby later, after we got on our feet financially. She agreed but was bitchy about not getting her way.

Our neighbor Q.T. Baker told me about an advertising manager position in the advertising department of Gibson's Department Stores in Abilene. The interview went very well because of my leverage from working at the agency. I said, "I couldn't possibly quit my present job for what they (Gibsons) were offering." I bluffed my way into starting at the fifth-year level for upper management. Their entry level position was more than what I was taking home from my paycheck at the agency. I started working at Gibson's producing two full pages of newspaper ads a week, from toothpaste to fishing tackle, plus radio and TV ads. It was a creative position. I hired a race car driver to visit the stores to promote new wheel rims. I found two jolly fellows to play Santa Claus at the two stores. We built a frontier store at the fairgrounds during rodeo season and stocked it with items sold at the stores. The position was filled with extra hours. Early on Sunday morning, I checked the newspaper ads and delivered them to the stores. I enjoyed the work and the manager position.

I was unbelievably excited to receive an acceptance letter to attend the art school at the Instituto in San Miguel. We made the decision to work nine more months, then move to Mexico so I could earn an Master's degree in Fine Arts. Audrey was excited about Mexico. She excelled in Spanish and was comfortable communicating in the language. To save money we lived in Dad's rent house, the former art gallery.

At work, when the store manager was absent, the assistant manager took the helm. He still cut his hair in a military buzz cut. He was a hot head, "X-Army", who liked to give me hell because I was a Marine. The office staff arrived an hour early before the floor personnel. The store was quiet except for the sound of typewriters and muffled conversations that floated over the partitions. A demonstration air horn in the hardware department was on the other side of the advertising office wall. "X-Army" blew the horn four mornings in a row sending me like a cartoon cat straight up in the air, claws sticking into the ceiling. I walked into "X-Army's" office and in a LOUD voice yelled, "I've asked you not to blow that horn for the last three days. You're an ass." I then expressed myself in more colorful language learned in the Corps. Flipping him the finger, I walked off the job.

These actions escalated our departure to Mexico. We immediately went to work selling our stuff, an old white

Ford truck, an ancient rabbit eared T.V., and several candle sticks from our wedding coddled in white tissue paper and their original white boxes. We sold everything we had and managed to scrape together $2,250. This was all we would have to live on for a year in Mexico. I asked Audrey's dad if he would loan us $50 a month while we were in school. He only acknowledged me with a cold, "NO". It felt like everyone didn't believe that we would succeed in Mexico. Charles told me, "You're crazy if you go to Mexico." Mother was very succinct, "Warren, you need to stay home and get a real job like driving a Mrs. Baird's Bread truck. You need to have job security with retirement benefits."

"Your achievements can be no greater than your PLANS are sound."
Mr. Hill

◈ CHAPTER NINE ◈

Moving to Mexico

"Get the facts before you act."
Dad

In the early fall of 1967 Audrey and I boarded a train in San Antonio, Texas with two trunks, three old suit cases and many cardboard boxes tied up like Christmas packages. I was wearing the blue suit, the one I wore often to the office. When I boarded, I was the only one wearing a suit. Four hours after crossing the Rio Grande, the Mexican authorities escorted us to their office on the train and demanded our entry papers. We only had our driver's licenses which were good at the border into Mexico, but not for the interior of the country. "Señor, you will be taken off the train at the next station and returned to the border for the proper papers." I stood up, grabbed my crotch, held up one finger and disappeared. I came back with a double handful of small packages of cigarettes saved from Marine Corps C-Rations, dumping them on the dark green table cloth with an ash tray that hadn't been emptied in days. I handed each officer a $5 bill, shook hands expressing appreciation and told them we were students going to San

Miguel de Allende. A long awkward moment followed, then the cigarette bribes were raked into their hats. The money disappeared. They motioned us out the door.

The next afternoon, the porter came down the aisle telling everyone we were arriving at the San Miguel station. I stepped off the train into a Clint Eastwood, spaghetti western movie set. The old station was dusty and the small ticket office antiquated. The building's plastered walls were crumbling. There weren't any people on the platform. The only thing the scene needed was a couple of tumbleweeds rolling through the station with music swelling into the opening scene of The Good, the Bad and the Ugly. Using my best Tex-Mex, I asked the porter, "Es este el correcto el estacion?" He assured me it was, but the town was eight miles away. The train started pulling away from the platform. I panicked, running around searching for our luggage because I couldn't see our boxes and trunks anywhere. Out of nowhere an old man pointed down the platform at our luggage stacked behind a partition. He was busy loading three large canvas mail pouches into a dust covered forty something Chevrolet with cracked windows. With a big smile, I waved a ten-dollar bill and signaled the mailman to load the car with our gear. We drove the eight miles to town with boxes sitting in our laps. It was ten dollars well spent. The mailman dropped us off at our hotel. Our belongings were stacked on the cobblestone street.

We were so excited; consequently, we didn't get much sleep. The next morning, we went looking for a place to live. We knocked on many doors. After lunch, a helpful stranger directed us to a large 10-foot-high white plastered wall with a blue wooden door. We rang the bell. A few minutes later a well-dressed gentleman opened the door onto a courtyard and greeted us in perfect English. We rented his guest house for $60 a month. To Audrey's delight, there were only twin beds. We looked out into a flower garden and orange grove. We had a commanding view of the bull ring and the pink Gothic church in the village center far below (Figure 20). We spent 25 cents on a taxi to haul our belongings up the cobblestone road to the top street above the village.

Figure 20: Pink gothic church in SanMiguel de Allende, Guanajuato, Mexico

After moving in, we wandered down the old streets and located the Instituto. We registered for classes which would start in three days. We were living in a fairy tale. The Instituto was down the hill, as was everything. On the way up, the hill became a mountain. Audrey registered for craft classes. I signed up for life drawing, painting, bronze sculpture and lithography. Now, I wanted specialized knowledge to become a professional artist. I attended art and Mexican history classes. Favorite teachers were, Señor Piñto (Spanish) painting, Detrick Kortlang (German) lithography, and Fred Samuelson (Texan) drawing. All the instructors were artists first and instructors second. They supplemented their income by teaching. They walked the talk. I learned techniques in drawing, painting, lithography, and sculpture (Figure 21).

Figure 21: Warren in Mexican studio, 1967

Arriving in San Miguel, nothing was familiar. Everything was new. We became intoxicated with the magic of Mexico. It was a kaleidoscope of impressions; the cobblestone streets, the 400-year-old, pink, gothic church, the festivals, the people, our market, the wood cutter who sold us our firewood and our maid. We paid her six dollars a week, a top wage, to cook our lunch, clean and go to the market for us. We visited Mexico City, toured the Aztec ruins of Tenochtitlan and became immersed in the culture. I attended classes, not for the grades, but because I really wanted to learn to be an artist. The stick of my curiosity was swung at the Mexican piñata. Out spilled the colorful traditions and adventures of living in a foreign country. I loved the Mexican lifestyle, the learning and creating art. Fellow students were Canadians, French, Italians, and Mexicans. In the second semester, I became the assistant to the lithography instructor and began working on my thesis in lithography (printing an image from a limestone slab). During lithography class, as many as three or four languages were spoken. It was exciting, and meaningful. Life was a candy store, a zoo, a circus and a rollercoaster ride all at the same time. Learning to be an artist was a daily experience in painting, sculpting and drawing. I had become a Mexican trained artist, plus I created a business. I bought used art supplies from students who were returning to their home countries and resold the supplies to new students. I turned a profit with my first customer. I was comfortable walking the cobblestone streets, going to art classes and taking the bus to other cities. I grew a beard, wore purple jeans and hiking boots. The ridiculous blue suit was never worn again.

The MFA degree from the Instituto took a year plus two additional summers. I gained a wealth of specialized knowledge. Before returning to the states we decided to take a bus trip to the Yucatan Peninsula to celebrate my MFA degree. We had enough money to buy third class everything for the three-week trip. On our way to visit the Mayan City of Uxmal in the Yucatan, a woman got on our crowded 3rd class bus and slid a metal bucket of fresh fish between my legs. A man then got on with a small jaguar in a cage made of sticks. Being poor in Mexico made traveling interesting. One night in Merida we found a place to stay for a few pesos. A former stable; our room with one bed, was a freshly painted bright yellow horse stall, complete with two swinging doors and no privacy.

We returned to San Miguel to pack up our art work and mementos for the train trip home. Our $2,250 budget bag had lasted down to the final few pesos for the year. I borrowed $8 in pesos from our neighbor across the street, so we could eat on the train. In the baggage car were boxes of drawings, lithographs, rolls of finished canvases, bronze sculptures and Audrey's craft work of silver jewelry, weavings and batik fabric. I lived a magical creative year in a foreign country and became a passionate student of art. Art would be my life's work.

The train slowed as we crossed the mud colored river of the Rio Grande. A sign proclaimed, "Welcome to the United States of America." The engine sounds of screeching, grinding and hissing finally came to a stop, but the engine continued to breathe steam in rhythm. I stepped off the train in the border town of Laredo, Texas to stretch. It would be a while before we reached San Antonio. I was on U.S. soil. The first thing I did was walk across the tracks to a vendor and buy a pack of Juicy Fruit gum. I handed the young woman a five peso note. She gave me change in American coins. I stood looking at the dime. It was so little. I had become Mexican and would now need to readjust to the U.S.A.

"There are two types of knowledge: General and Specialized. Specialized Knowledge that is organized and directed will assist you in obtaining your goals.

Seek out Specialized Knowledge! Develop your skills so that you can be all you want to be. Sharpen your expertise. The more specialized knowledge you have, the more others will seek you out."

Mr. Hill

◈ CHAPTER TEN ◈

University Art Instructor

"If you want something bad enough, go after it."
Dad

Returning from Mexico, I applied for university teaching positions. In the meantime I got my old job back working at Etheridge Survey Company for a dollar an hour. The job was cutting site line for the surveyor. I had loaded the pickup for the day's work and had finished sharpening the axes when Mr. Etheridge came out on the office porch and told me, "Warren you have a phone call."

"Hello, this is Warren Cullar, yes sir, yes sir, thank you sir, good bye." I yelled at Mr. Etheridge and the two other crew members, "I got the university job." Congratulations all around. I could not smile any wider. I daydreamed in the truck for the hour drive to the survey site. The job was a future lake site near Breckenridge, Texas. I chopped spiny mesquite trees all day, lost in the thought of being assistant professor of art at Hardin Simmons University. Orientation would be in three weeks. This was the time to meet the university staff and professors. I was extremely happy for many reasons. I proved "Them" wrong again.

The "out of country degree" I had earned in Mexico had been accepted for a university teaching position.

We rented a small house across the street from the university, a short walk to the art department. I enjoyed the students and spent a lot of time at the university painting and improving my teaching ability. When I received the position at Hardin Simmons University, Audrey enrolled to finish a year or so of college credits. Her tuition was very expensive and our money was scarce. Again, she was pushing me to have a baby. I said, "We can't afford a baby on my meager salary, you need to finish college, then let's talk about it." She agreed.

Months later at the beginning of the second year of teaching, Audrey waited until we were at her parent's home for Sunday dinner. She announced to my surprise that she was pregnant. My mouth fell open, "You broke our agreement to wait." She only glared at me. She had obviously quit taking birth control pills. She told me she was on the pill. What a liar! She only wanted to replace the baby taken away from her. I felt left out of a major decision. Me or my opinions meant nothing. From then on, sex was only to keep me in line. She controlled me by letting me get in between her ever-growing thighs. Sex was terrible. She started eating on our honeymoon, I watched her take a finger and clean out an avocado bowl. She gained sizes in her jeans and put on the pounds.

I went off to work in a tie and sports jacket as was expected. Audrey wore knee high leather fringed boots, jeans two sizes too tight, a loose un-ironed blouse and her hair in pigtails with no makeup. That dress style was ok in Mexico as students, but as the wife of a university professor it was unacceptable. I was not happy in the marriage, I was embarrassed to be seen with Audrey, but stupidly faithful. She told me she didn't have to wear makeup because she was married. Even her Mother told her more than once to wash her hair. I was miserable. I buried myself in extra work at the office and dreaded to come home. There was no love in our rented house. Our relationship and everything else felt cold and uncomfortable. I was in a make-believe world. I found an antique bassinet and spent disproportionate periods of time cleaning, sanding and painting. I worked in the yard and bought a bee hive to observe the bees; anything to keep me occupied. It was alright with Audrey. She didn't even pay attention. She sat sideways in an old cloth covered rocker. She would sling her legs over the arm and read her romance novels for hours. She was content. She was getting exactly what she wanted; a baby on the way.

Because of religious doctrine I accepted my fate. I didn't own up to the idea until much later that I was only used as a legal stud service to do the job. After that I was as useless as a male spider copulating with a Black Widow. After he impregnates the female Black Widow, she eats him. I felt exactly like I was being eaten alive.

The routine at the art department was to finish the first class and get a coffee at the student union. It was a place where I could talk with the students. Sometimes I sat in the patio of the art department, especially in nice weather to enjoy a cup of coffee. The trees and ivy-covered buildings created a real collegiate atmosphere. One morning on the way for coffee, I scanned a letter on the bulletin board announcing the opening of a new two-year college in Snyder, Texas about an hour and half away. It listed instructors' positions, including two in the art department. I was waiting in line for coffee and the thought occurred to me to call about the position.

Back in the office, I dialed President Clinton in Snyder, Texas. “This is Robert Clinton; how may I help you?” Dad always told me, if you want to get someone’s attention, talk to their interest. “Dr. Clinton, this is Warren Cullar and I’m an art instructor at Hardin Simmons University. I’m interested in the new college you're building.” Dr. Clinton’s voice and the vision revealed his passion. In fifteen minutes, he articulated a concise overview of the college, specifically, the plans for the art department. He asked me if I had any more questions. “No sir! I have only one request! I want the position!” He laughed, I knew I had the job. A week later I received a large envelope. In it was an overview of the college and an application for a teaching position. I put it in the mail the next morning. After three weeks, I received a phone call from Dr. Brock, Dean of Faculty. He asked if he and Dr. Clinton could observe my classes. I informed my students that special guests would be visiting and I needed student cooperation. We cleaned the art rooms and organized the work to best display their talents. Even Mr. Stokes, the janitor, did his part. By show time we were ready. I opened the art building early Wednesday. Two hours later the department secretary escorted two gentlemen into the office. I shook hands with Dr. Clinton and Dr. Brock, exactly as Dad had taught me. I made sure that I looked directly into their eyes. I gave a brief tour of the art department. Class started. Confidence and excitement were flowing through me. By the third class I noticed the guests had gone. One of the students said they had gone out for coffee and would be back. The day finished, I smiled inside and out. We were a success.

The community of Snyder was an oil boom town. I

received an invitation to attend the opening of a wealthy oil man's private art collection. I attended and met many of the college board members. At the afternoon's end Dr. Clinton invited me to his home and presented me with a contract to sign. I had passed all the hurdles for the position. I drove home with the contract on the front seat and a four thousand dollar increase over the current HSU contract. Yes!

Audrey, the baby, and I drove to Snyder. We found an antique house by knocking on doors and asking questions. I purchased, a real "fix-er-upper," on the wrong side of the tracks, but the price was right at $4,000. A loan from the teacher's credit union sealed the deal.

The college was a construction zone with only piles of dirt and foundations, so I went to work. The president handed me the plans for the art department and asked for suggestions. The position included creating the art curriculum, purchasing all art supplies and buying art books for the library. I was to travel to area high schools and recruit art students by offering scholarships. I would teach the classes. Snyder's tax base was from oil, lots of oil, so the small two-year college had the money to create a handsome campus in the middle of nowhere. The first year, I spent sixty plus hours a week working, getting the studios into an operational college art department. The students in the beginning classes assembled the easels. We held classes in the Methodist church fellowship hall. It took a few months for the campus to take on the look and function of a two-year college.

"Fortunes gravitate to men whose minds have been prepared to 'attract' them, just as surely as water gravitates to the ocean."
Mr. Hill

◈ CHAPTER ELEVEN ◈

Divorced & Married for Love

"Live each day as if it were your last."
Dad

Friday afternoon, my life-long friend Russ picked me up in Snyder and we drove to Santa Fe, New Mexico. He was applying for a job working as a set designer for the Santa Fe Opera. We both had chosen the field of art. He graduated from California College of Arts and Crafts and I from the Instituto de Allende. We had been friends since he moved in across the alley when I was 9 and he was 8. We spent almost equal time at each other's home. I remember his dad and mom with affection. He called my parents Mr. C and Mrs. C. As kids, we rode our bikes to the creek and caught one bite perch for Dad to pan fry in an old skillet. Mother always made a fuss about the smell. In high school Russ drove a '50 model Ford. Mine was a '49 Ford. We doubled dated. He became the art editor for the Abilene High year book. His parents helped him financially through college. During his sophomore year he was t-boned driving his Volkswagen and was injured from head to toe. I visited him in Abilene where he was confined to a wheel chair, eventually graduating to crutches. Today he sometimes uses a cane. One eyelid still droops a little. He never complained then or now.

We would return from New Mexico by Sunday night so I wouldn't miss any classes. The afternoon sun was painting red and purple streaks across the western sky as we arrived in Santa Fe. After some Mexican food and an art gallery opening, I was ready to hit the pillow. I was tired and complaining as we climbed the worn brown carpeted stairs to the second floor of the shabby hotel. He took the bed close to the window, where the glare of the neon hotel sign lit the shade to a Coca Cola red. My bed had a thin white spread on an old black metal bed frame. A rickety vanity and wicker rocking chair completed the furnishings. Saturday, he went to his interview. I enjoyed tourist status and visited gallery after gallery.

That night after dinner Russ wanted to go to a bar. This kind of experience was not me. I didn't drink beer because my taste buds had no desire, and besides it cost money. We occupied a little round table in the Senate Lounge a block from the New Mexico state capital. My hand was wrapped around a warm can of beer. Russ was dancing.

I looked up as two young women entered the bar; I picked the short busty blond with long hair. I stood up and jumped over a two-foot railing separating the tables from the dance floor. "Would you like to join us?" Introductions were made and we sat down again. I was mesmerized. "She" radiated beauty and her blue eyes danced in the lights. Donna lived in Pueblo, Colorado. She and her good friend "Coots", who was a nurse, had driven down for the weekend. We kept on talking until the bar closed at one.

Back at my hotel Donna sat in the only chair in the

room. It was a comfortable rocker. I sat on the floor. I had no interest in a one-night stand. We talked until three, then I walked her across the square to her hotel. I did not tell her I was married and had a child. (Like my father, I didn't wear my wedding ring except on special occasions. He did it because of safety on the job. I just didn't like wearing a ring.) I wrote the address of the college on the bar receipt and handed it to her. I gave her one long hug and said good bye. Walking through the deserted tree covered square with the glare of the orange street lights, I spoke to the silence, "I didn't kiss her."

The next morning on the way out of town, Russ and I stopped at Dunkin Donuts for coffee. I called Donna from a pay phone. Her voice was soft and musical, I said, "I enjoyed meeting you and loved our stimulating conversation that lasted until almost four in the morning." A few more words were exchanged, then a simple, "Good Bye." Russ didn't talk much on the six-hour drive. Lost and dreaming in my mind, I replayed meeting Donna. Any future thoughts about her were unfortunately out of the question, I was obligated, I was married.

The following weekend I went to Dallas with two newly hired instructors. Each had an independent mission. My mission was to select a decorative water feature for the campus. I purchased the appropriate fountain and completed shipping arrangements. The three of us went for dinner, I excused myself from the table and found a quiet place to use the pay phone in the lobby. I called Donna. She was excited to hear from me. During the first part of the call I said to her, "I was not truthful the night we met. I am married, but not happy." She asked, "Are there children?" I told her about the daughter. We talked for a long time.

When I got home, Audrey met me at the door waving a card, demanding to know what it was about. She had opened my mail at the college. I grabbed the card out of her hand and read the card. It was a cartoon of a lion and it only said "You're Grrreat! signed, Donna." Audrey said, "Well what about this?" shoving the card in my face. Without thinking, I fired back "IT'S A DIVORCE!" I never said another word concerning the card or anything about the trip to Santa Fe.

Strangely, Audrey never asked any more questions. I think she was as finished with me as I was with her. She agreed quickly to a divorce. I had never been in love with Audrey and I was miserable living with her. Her mother ordered her father around and Audrey copied her mother's style. I lived with her for the last six weeks of the semester. We planned an exit and a divorce. We didn't have much to say or divide. I paid her half the value of the house and half the value of the car. We also divided our joint account. I agreed to sign over the deed to the 5 acres, plus of course, child support for the baby.

Packing felt final. Breaking away from Audrey's tension created a feeling of freedom. The divorce would be completed in August. I traded watercolors for the lawyer's services. The dented used Datsun station wagon was loaded with painting supplies, a new portable easel and a suitcase. The next morning, I taught the last class, turned in some paper work at the college office and drove out of Texas toward Colorado. Since the announcement of "It's a divorce" I had talked to Donna often. The anticipation of seeing Donna intensified. Excitement was replaced with weariness as I pulled into a truck stop after hours of driving. I slept in the car. I took a shower, shaved and had a breakfast made for truck drivers.

I was ready to drive over Raton Pass into Colorado.

Mid-afternoon I arrived in Pueblo. Donna was driving in from a meeting in Denver and would not arrive until five. I found the public library and settled into a comfortable chair among the art stacks. Fretfully, I thumbed through a variety of books. A book, "West" by Peter McIntire, captivated me because it was a British artist painting on location in the western United States. I thought, "That's what I want to do sometime. Oh! Wow! It's 5:30 already!"

Donna's apartment was difficult to find. At last, I knocked on her door. She opened the door smiling. I took her in my arms and kissed her, mumbling something about being so glad to see her. We stood in the doorway kissing; both of us on fire. She giggled and said, "Would you like to come in?" She led me to the bedroom and there we made hot love. That night we walked to a near-by restaurant for pizza. We sat in a booth and held hands. The energy from holding her hand was electrifying, I was in love.

Donna worked as a public relationship specialist for the National Dairy Council. She would go to her office downtown and I would spend the day painting. On weekends, we packed lunch and drove into the mountains with a destination of another ghost town. I set up my easel and painted watercolors. She found a shady place to read. It was a romantic summer of sharing and learning. The weeks sped by. With tears which were both happy and sad, we parted with plans to meet at Christmas.

I drove back to Snyder and opened the antique oval glass door. The August heat blew out the smell of stinking garbage from under the sink. The refrigerator was missing, I had installed it flush with the wall, it had been pried out with a crowbar. Audrey's agreement to divide things in our house had been annihilated. All that was left were my clothes hanging in the closet, (some in a pile on the floor) two folding canvas chairs and 4 jelly glasses. The reason she didn't take the canvas chairs was because when she stood up the chair attached to her big butt. Knowing her, I don't know why she didn't take the 4 jelly glasses.

I didn't care because I was single, and with the help of my brother Charles we remodeled the house. The house was almost finished by Christmas when Donna came from Colorado to meet my parents. They instantly loved her, especially Dad. In late spring on Easter Sunday, I asked Donna to marry me. We married in Denver, Colorado August 30th, 1972. I was 30 and she was 25.

After a brief move and honeymoon, we set up housekeeping in Snyder. It had been a magical year of romance, marriage, painting in the ghost towns of Colorado and moving Donna to Snyder. It was the start of my third-year teaching at Western Texas College.

At the request of friend Jerry Baird who wanted to see the summer paintings, Donna and I held our first art show in our living room. I had a tripod easel with a clamp on light and 9 framed watercolors. We served pie and coffee to three couples and sold 3 paintings. While not exactly the same as how I sell art today, people still like to be entertained, educated, fed and sold.

"You may be hurt if you love too much, but you will live in misery if you love too little."
Mr. Hill

◈ CHAPTER TWELVE ◈

A Money Goal

"Treat yourself to 'Good Thoughts' for the day."
Dad

The grinding whirl of the sharpener sculpted another #2 yellow pencil. I doodled on a white 3"x 5" card. I was reflecting on the growth of my income. It's 1975, and I'm holding office hours at Western Texas College in Snyder, Texas. In 1966, I was making $1.50 an hour as a commercial artist. In 1969, as a young art instructor at Hardin Simmons University, my salary was a little over $5,000 a year. Now, 1975, I was making $13,000 a year at Western Texas College for a nine-month contract (Figure 22).

I supported us on my salary along with money from the sale of my watercolors. Summer and weekends, I painted watercolors at a card-table studio located in the corner of the kitchen/dining room of our wood-frame home. I painted our house a Canary yellow with lime green trim. One old curmudgeon wanted to know why I didn't paint the house white like most sensible people. I'm sure, to his relief, after we sold the house, the new buyers re-painted it white.

We paid off our modest home with the extra income

from holding art parties every couple of months to sell watercolors. I wanted to do more than just pay the bills. I was going to have to think bigger. I had *Think and Grow Rich* on my desk. I needed a new goal, a dollar amount. I picked out a number and penciled it on a 3"x 5" card.

Figure 22: Teaching at Western Texas College, Snyder, Texas, 1973

I pinned the note to the cork board above my desk. I folded my arms, leaned back in the chair and took a long look at the new goal. The number made a gigantic impact. I visualized how life would feel. More income would develop a better lifestyle.

The college dean knocked on the door frame of my office. He was checking on his troops for a future staff meeting. He noticed the $40,000 goal note stapled to the cork board (Figure 23). I remember his smirking face and his comment about how impossible it would be for me to earn that much in one year. The goal was certainly more than his present salary. I calmly said, "I will make the $40,000 in four years and more every year after that." He mumbled something under his breath and left my office.

Figure 23: The $40,000 Goal

"Whatever the mind of man can conceive and believe, it can achieve. There are no limitations to the mind except those we acknowledge."
Mr. Hill

◈ CHAPTER THIRTEEN ◈

Resigned & Cullar Gallery

"Get good at a few things."
Dad

The West Texas wind caught the door of the Snyder Art Club building. The door slammed open with the rattling sound of metal on metal. A bald man, in a bright yellow shirt, wearing black horn-rimmed glasses, stumbled into the room along with a blast of sand. Bud Biggs, the workshop instructor, clutched his hat and an armload of painting supplies.

It was 1972 and I had just witnessed the entrance of the man who would become my mentor and friend. There was a twinkle in his eyes and a mischievous smile. The chairman of the art club introduced me as one of the art instructors from the College. Bud walked up, extended his hand and looked me straight in the eye. Both of us were the same height. I told him I knew a little about watercolor, but I wanted to learn more. Bud's brush twirled in the air as he turned and caught it behind his back for fun. He expected his students to perform and perform they did. The next few years I continued to take his beginning watercolor classes. We painted on location together and had long conversations about painting and life. Mostly we laughed a lot (Figure 24).

Figure 24: Artist Bud Biggs

Watching him paint was exciting. I painted the subject as close to how he executed the watercolor as possible. He called me "little brother". One afternoon he told me, "Warren, if you can learn to 'paint behind', you'll be a great watercolorist." I learned how to paint a positive image using negative space. He taught me the special skills he had acquired over a lifetime as a commercial artist and watercolorist. Bud loved watercolor painting and that transferred to me. I was painting at home and teaching at the college.

One morning at the college, a fellow who oversaw the facility correspondence asked me if I wanted to go to Egypt on an educational grant, I said "YES." I had wanted to go to Egypt since Dr. Sasser's freshmen class in Ancient Architecture. I took the application down to President Clinton's office. Mrs. Martin motioned for me to go in. Dr. Clinton read the application, I told him of my desire to visit Egypt. The grant was for six weeks the following summer. The first hurdle was a nomination for the grant from the college. There were 90 candidates. 17 would be selected for the grant team. Dad always said, "If you want the best information, go to the source."

I called the director of the grant, Mr. Bryan. After a few minutes of conversation, I asked, "Mr. Bryan, what type of research do you have in mind for the art area?" He replied, "Interview the staff of the Papyrus Institute in Cairo. Write a paper to describe the process. Take photographs of the production of papyrus paper. Ultimately, create a slide presentation."

The ancient Egyptians had used the Nile River plant for 5000 years to make paper. With a couple of hours of library research, I orchestrated a plan to match the director's vision. I combined his ideas with mine. I got the grant. Saying good bye to Donna was the difficult part, I was concerned that she would be alone for weeks, but Dad said they would see her often.

On arrival in Egypt traffic moved at snail speed from the airport into downtown Cairo. It was a cacophony of cars, trucks, camels, carts and motor cycles that belched clouds of blue tail pipe exhaust. Vendors added their own chorus of yells, holding up strings of flowers, light bulbs, even fly swatters. I just wanted it all to stop. Exhaustion, hunger and a headache put me in a fetal position. We arrived at the hotel at 2 am. I pulled the spread off the bed and collapsed. I woke to the same sounds from the night before echoing off the pavement five stories below. Egypt in 1975 was a combination of poverty and lost hopes. War with Israel had depleted everything and signs of a third world country were everywhere. Six weeks didn't seem like a long time, until the end of the first week, when the novelty of Egypt had worn off. I missed Donna. In the early morning hours, I was vulnerable to thoughts of her. I missed her touch and warmth, I crushed the pillow into a Donna shape and imagined her in bed with me. I remembered how her hair smelled when I nuzzled the back of her neck and how my hand cupped her breast. Sleep was sketchy. Only the faint glow of dawn told me I had survived another night. The curtain on this drama opened almost every night except when I was too tired for erotic thoughts. Sleep came then as a relief.

The desert's afternoon sun was low. Swirling sandy air turned the sun into a hammer of white hot metal. I was drinking a Heineken on the hotel's roof top bar. I leaned back in my metal chair and took a long look at the watercolor I was painting. I glanced toward the western horizon. I could see the familiar pyramids. They reminded me of Dad who would give me a quarter and send me running to the grocery store for a pack of Camels. The pack of cigarettes had a picture of three pyramids, a palm tree and a camel. Memory had become reality.

My six-week Egyptian study grant was over, I was ready to go home. I had completed a research paper on the Papyrus Institute and the process of paper making. I had toured the delta, the Sinai and visited the

Valley of the Kings. I had seen the Pyramids, temples, tombs and eaten my way up and down the length of the Nile. I used every mode of transportation: airplane, train, camel, donkey, horse cart, felucca (ancient sailing ship) plus a sometimes air conditioned mini bus.

The peak moment of the trip came when we traveled deep into the sand dunes near Alexandria. We passed Bedouin black tents and stopped at a rather informal home among a few palm trees. A helicopter was parked a short distance away. There was nothing but high sand for 360 degrees. We piled out of the hot van. A guard in a starched uniform opened a small wooden blue gate and we filed down a path. On the porch, I shook hands with a tall gentleman sporting a distinguished mustache, I said "Good afternoon." I stepped inside and then realized, I had shaken hands with Egyptian President, Anwar Sadat. We were all served the traditional hot Karkade (Hibiscus tea) in small glasses. The President of Egypt leaned back in his chair, packed his pipe and asked if we had questions. I asked the last question that wrapped up our conversation. "Mr. President, what may we do to assist you in creating your country into a nation of peace in the Middle East?" He spoke, "When you return to America please tell (your citizens) that your Egyptian friends sincerely want peace." The hour of Q&A ended, and he suggested we go outside for photographs. As I walked out on the porch, I suddenly realized, I was thinking and acting as a foreign diplomat.

I took a sip of beer and let out an exhausted sigh. I was homesick for Donna. I was completing the last watercolor of the dozen I had managed to paint during our busy study trip. Tomorrow, all 17 team members would leave Cairo and fly to Dallas. I finished reading Donna's two-week-old letter. She wrote that we had an invitation to visit Bud and Maggie in Dallas after I got home. Bud, my watercolor instructor, mentor and friend! The thrill of going home kept me turning in the bed covers until five am. The flight was long. At the Dallas airport, Donna was nowhere to be found, I searched for several minutes. I took a seat then waited. A person coughed behind me. I stood up, turned and looked into Donna's beautiful face. In unison we said, "How long have you been sitting there?" Both of us missed each other in the waiting area and we had been sitting back to back for thirty minutes. I hugged her. I told her that I would never leave her for that long again.

On the way home, I noticed how blue the Texas sky was and the vegetation so green. The Egyptian sky was always a sand color, never blue. In downtown Cairo, all the trees were covered with a dusting from the desert. We shared our news. I asked if she knew the decision of the college committee for a raise in my rank. Her frown told the story. The college faculty had denied the raise. She said, "The report stated you were spending too much time on art and not enough involvement with the students." I was insulted and hurt. Their decision negated all the 4 years of work I had put into the college. I was there from the beginning to start the art department. I taught the students by demonstrating drawing techniques, watercolor, and 2D design. I enjoyed the students and the work they produced. Donna and I talked about how I was always in the spotlight, taking students out to tour the Santa Fe galleries. I created contests that got more students involved. To top it all off, I was selling watercolors and everyone knew it. After I donated several to the library. Donna said, "Can't you see that all the outside work you and your students create is written up in the newspaper along with photos. Your work is causing jealously among the faculty. Think of it! Does the English department get any publicity like that?" I replied, "I guess not." She continued, "Besides, you just got back from a six-week trip to Egypt. Don't you think that upset some of the instructors?" I recognized that I was slowly being squeezed out.

A week before the semester started, we drove to Dallas to visit artist Bud and his wife Maggie. Bud had converted their spacious living room into a painting classroom. Their ranch style home had big rooms. The living room had three large picture windows across the north side, perfect for painting. He had installed a hanging mirror at an angle above his painting table so that all the students could see his pallet and his movements painting. Narrow fold up tables were set in four rows of seven students. Classes were held twice a week. Getting in as a new student was impossible because he was such an extraordinary instructor. He taught with a lot of laughter.

One quiet Saturday afternoon in his studio, there were just the two of us. I sat on a tall stool to his right to see his mixing tray and to watch him paint. His brush moved across the paper like a conductor directing an orchestra. Our conversation was about painting, workshops and my disappointment with the college. I told him about the politics and the recent developments of being turned down for a raise in rank. He stopped painting, hesitated for a moment and took a deep breath. He put his brush in the water can, swirled the brush to clean the paint out of it and laid it down on a towel. He looked over his glasses right in my face and said, **"Warren, don't wait until you're my age to paint full-time."** I was stunned. His words were more like a command than a conversation. It was the same overpowering feeling I had when Dad broke my plate. I was about to ask him about being a full-time painter, but our wives interrupted us with armloads of shopping bags. He dipped his brush into the water can and continued to paint. I had not thought of being a full-time artist because of my salary and three months off to travel and paint. I had a pretty sweet deal. His words, "Don't wait" kept me thinking. That night I watched the clock from 1:19 am until 3:23 am. I drifted off to restless sleep.

The next afternoon, during the four-hour drive home, I expressed disappointment to Donna about how the college administration was not appreciating the work I was doing for the students and the college. I told her about the conversation with Bud and his command to be a full-time artist now. I remember asking her, "What do you think of me becoming full-time?" She replied, "Warren, if you really want to be an artist I will be 100% behind you. I will help you, but I am a little scared." I said, "Our car is paid for, and our home is almost, so we can afford the risk." Donna said, "We will be debt free before you become a full-time artist." When I heard, her say "full-time artist", I knew the truth was spoken. The decision was made.

As we drove into our driveway, I couldn't wait to write a letter of resignation to the college dean. I weighed the pros and cons. The scale tipped toward becoming an artist. Brother Charles had moved to Snyder because I had heard of a position at city hall that fit him and suggested he apply. Donna helped him write his resume and he was hired. He had an office in city hall, a secretary and a city car. He wore several different hats of responsibility. He had not been supportive of my past decisions, but this time I told him about the circumstances and his advice fit perfectly. "Warren, you have a contract for the next nine months. Finish it and use the time to prepare, but I still think you're crazy to try to make a living as an artist." I saw myself as an artist and began the transition out of teaching. Producing art consumed every available moment. I needed dozens of finished watercolors before I could hang out the "ARTIST" shingle.

Spring break, Donna and I were on the way as exhibitors to our first outdoor art show in San Antonio, Texas. We drove through the Texas Hill Country on an April day, with the spring bluebonnets blooming in azure waves across the fields. It was a magnificent sight for folks that lived in dry West Texas. We passed an old farmhouse surrounded by a grove of giant oak trees. The property, east of Bertram, was a bouquet of tall hollyhocks and bluebonnets and had a "For Sale" sign nailed to the gatepost. We both said, "Let's go back!"

The gravel crunched under the weight of our tires as Donna and I slowly drove up the driveway under the shade of a majestic 200-year-old live oak. Its branches towered over a newer building that begged to be converted into an art gallery. We walked onto the long cement porch of this turn-of-the-century house and peered into the empty rooms. I said to Donna, "Look at the Hill Country view from the porch –wow!" She smiled.

The panoramic view was breathtaking. To the west was a windmill (Figure 25) with greenery that rolled away to the south. The new building was to the east out by the highway.

The scene was a painting in 3D. We absorbed the view: trees, bluebonnets, and our future art gallery. An hour later we made an appointment for Monday. The realtor told us the price was $27,000 for the two buildings on three acres.

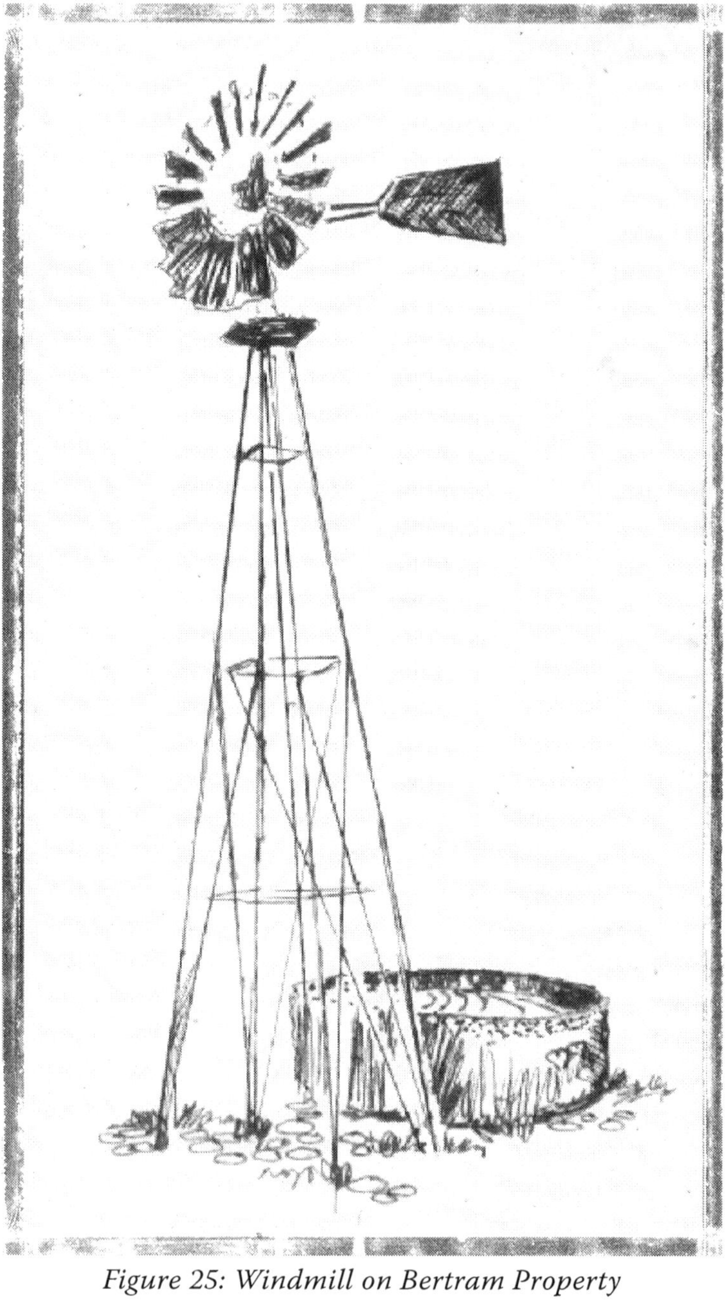

Figure 25: Windmill on Bertram Property

We arrived in San Antonio and registered for the downtown art fair. This show was our first art fair. Our set up included a piece of plastic, four poles, some rope and a pair of upside down TV tables. The display held four stuffed cardboard portfolios of matted watercolors painted during my years of teaching. The watercolors were class demonstrations that I had painted for the students. Our booth was along the beautiful River Walk at the Starving Artist Show. Nothing there could be sold for over $10.

We had no idea what to expect until the first couple arrived. They flipped through our portfolios and selected three matted watercolors. Donna collected $30. People began standing in line holding $10 bills in their hands and watercolors under their arms. After the first day we were exhausted, excited, and hungry. We closed-down our makeshift booth, returned the almost empty portfolios to the old station wagon and found a place under the seat to stash the wads of cash. We treated ourselves to a well-deserved celebratory dinner. We repeated the art sales the next day until our inventory was almost gone.

We moved into the new home in Bertram on May 8th, 1976, along with our very pregnant cat, Lady Jane Grey. Our caravan of Donna, Brother Charles and his wife Vicki, took six hours. We unloaded the rent- a- truck into the gallery building under pouring rain. I began to wonder if I had made a big mistake. The old fear factor waiting to sabotage me lurked behind any risk-taking experience, if I allowed it. Like Cortez in the Bay of Veracruz, when he had his ships burned and told his men they would either conquer Mexico or die on the beach, I too had no choice. I would turn this old farm house and former café into a great home and gallery.

We created another plan right out of Hill's book, *Think*

and Grow Rich. His main points had become second nature. For three months, we slept on a mattress on a stack of sheetrock. The refrigerator was in the living room and we ate on a picnic table. Weeks of work turned the country farm house into a comfortable home and the café became a gallery and a space for workshop students. We were ready to open. I proudly cut the Cullar Gallery logo out of plywood and attached it to the front of the new gallery fence. Bud had given me the suggestion to become a full-time artist. Now was the beginning of that journey.

Yes, we had an impressive three acres and a dozen giant live oaks that had stood on that spot for hundreds of years. The native Americans that moved through the cedars following the wildlife, camped among those ancient oaks. They witnessed the first white settlers and watched them dig a cistern that still worked. The two-room log cabin had long ago disappeared and the new house and wind mill were built in 1902. In the 60's the café was added. In 1976 the artist and his wife had arrived. They had cleaned the space, planted a garden and remodeled the buildings, and put up a sign "Cullar Gallery". September 11th, 1976 was our opening. Over a hundred people came because of the two-full page newspaper interview with photos. Our new neighbors drank ice tea, ate snacks and watched me paint a watercolor. The celebration lasted all afternoon with tours of the house and gallery. I did not make a sale.

Georgetown, Texas was down the road and old friend Bud was scheduled to conduct another watercolor workshop about six months after we opened our gallery. Donna mailed my tuition to the watercolor club. Bud and Maggie came for a visit the day before the workshop. We spent the afternoon visiting, drinking glacial cold tea and munching on watermelon. We enjoyed each other's company with the shade and breeze. A lone buzzard circled the ultramarine sky dotted with popcorn clouds. I showed off our home and studio/gallery. I could tell Bud was proud of our accomplishments. I had incorporated his knowledge and skills to become a full-time artist. Bud had instilled in me the concept and drive to become a full-time artist by his simple statement that changed my career course forever.

"Knowledge is only potential power. It becomes power only when, and if, it is organized into definitive plans of action, and directed to a definite end."
Mr. Hill

◈ CHAPTER FOURTEEN ◈

I Became a Real Artist

"Plan for a rainy day."
Dad

In May of 1976 we arrived in Bertram with retirement funds from the college and money from selling three houses that brother Charles and I had remodeled. That money plus art sales totaled $30,000. We wrote a large down payment check when we purchased our Bertram home and spent a considerable amount remodeling. We worked diligently to advance our income. After a year, our roadside "fruit stand" art gallery on Highway 29, east of Bertram, Texas, had a slow leak in the money tire. We were not making enough to get us jump-started down the road to financial success. We needed an infusion of cash. We weren't broke, but we were down to the last few hundred dollars in the bottom of the Mason jar.

January 5th, 1977 was 16 months after we had opened the gallery. I packed art gear as the wind at the corner of the house howled like a coyote on a stormy night. With the back seat of the AMC Pacer folded down, I managed to magically squeeze in a dozen framed watercolors, boxes of post cards and a portable easel. I had everything I needed to lecture and do a demonstration painting. Donna came out on the porch and handed me a blanket. She said, "Honey, please put this behind the seat so I can keep warm on our drive." We left the next afternoon on a drive to a watercolor group meeting. We had a good chance of selling the framed paintings and certainly the demonstration painting.

Most watercolor organizations did not have a budget to pay a fee for a lecture and demonstration, so we created a two-hour watercolor demonstration for art organizations around the state. The objective was to present FREE demonstrations only in the month of January. We believed what you give, comes back to you in ways you can't even imagine. We presented our first demonstrations the year before. Now we had a following of watercolor clubs and a schedule of 16 watercolor demonstrations in Texas. It made for a very busy start to the new year. A Texas Blue Norther was blowing with bone chilling wrath, making life miserable. Our second appointment was scheduled in the arts and crafts department on the Army base at Fort Hood, north of our Bertram home. The Army had requested our presentation and had publicized our event. We had to make the trip, show up, lecture and paint a demonstration watercolor.

As we backed out of the driveway, the bitter wind bent the tree branches like witches on Halloween brooms, mocking our escape. Storm clouds, streaming low to the ground, raced to beat us to the county line. We took a dirt road shortcut, saving a couple dozen miles, but our anguish increased as the car shimmied against the blasting, frigid air. The drive took longer than expected. Finding the location was like a crazy Monolopy® game. DO NOT PASS GO! The Army Base's arts and crafts department was in

Figure 26: "Nighthawks" by Edward Hopper

a chilly basement. The heat had not been turned up and no coffee was available. The dozen or so art enthusiasts were sentenced to tall wooden stools for the presentation. They looked uncomfortable. I visualized them wearing pointed dunce caps. My hands were frozen from unloading the equipment. I did a fair watercolor demo and my concluding remarks were still hanging in the air, like frozen sheets in the wind, as the entire ensemble disappeared into the cold, black night. The deck was stacked against us. We didn't make a dime. Not one sale; not even a set of post cards for a dollar! I folded the easel, packed the dozen framed watercolors, and we slowly drove off the base.

I found an all-night café. It looked like the painting "Nighthawks" by Edward Hopper (Figure 26). We ordered two coffees served in mugs like the ones I once found in an old shed behind my grandfather's house. The mugs were white, thick ceramic, aged like ancient Chinese porcelains, with cracks and patinas indicating years of hunkered over conversations (Figure 27). We were participating in the same ceremony, but no talk... only the clinking of the spoons in our coffee mugs. We sat depressed and out of energy. Our backs were against the wall. We were out of options. I looked at Donna, managed a weak smile and said: "We need a miracle." Disappointment was in her eyes. She was tired and we both were exhausted after the struggle of working and watching our resources slowly circle down in a whirlpool of desperation.

Figure 27: Ceramic coffee mugs

The coffee, especially the second refill, propelled us into the coldest night of any January in years. I opened the car for Donna. She said, "Let's talk, OK!" By the time, I unlocked the car and started the engine Donna said quietly, "Let's start over, with new ideas." I replied, "Yes, we have everything in place. There's our home, the studio is organized, and we have several art shows scheduled for the spring and summer. What do we need to add?" Donna said, "We have to start from scratch and do something totally different." I was thinking out loud, "I know we have never produced prints, but what if we sold a collection of prints to our collectors at a discount?"

Our car and ideas raced the wind on the way home. We were soon engaged in a caffeine charged conversation about a new plan. In the driveway, I killed the engine. We sat in dark silence for a few moments. In only one hour and forty-seven minutes, from café to driveway, we had developed our plan. We were excited; hopeful. I opened the front door. The house was frigid, so I brought in wood and quickly started a fire. We cuddled up on the couch with hot mint tea, ending a very long day.

Early sunlight streamed into the studio. I selected a painting from the arsenal of finished watercolors to be the first print. Our organized plan was simple. We would sell one hundred collectors a series of ten prints for a discount price of $100. We named our plan "THE FIRST 100". One print would be published every four months. The collectors would pay $100 in advance before I painted or released the remaining watercolors. Others would pay the retail price of $250 for all 10 images.

Our plan was a calculated risk, gambling on our imagination. Energy in motion, we started calling collectors. By six weeks, 100 collectors paid $10,000, plus $2,500 from sales of the 16 watercolor society's demonstrations. Traveling, lecturing, painting and selling during January and February 1977 took all our energy. Our Mason jar totaled $12,500. A loose budget was drawn up for the new-found treasure. We set aside money for publishing the first three prints, living expenses, a rainy-day fund and a future investing fund. The masterminding of the "First 100" developed out of a desire to create money. In March, we printed the first of ten prints in an edition of 750. Eventually ten prints would equal a total of 7500 prints, starting at $25 each. The prices would escalate as the print editions sold.

We were home and finished with traveling. I walked out on the porch, turned up my collar, pulled on a sock hat and leather gloves. Stopping at the wood pile, between two live oaks, I stacked up an arm load. I felt cold wet drops as I walked across the drive. I pushed open the front door and announced to Donna, "We're going to need more firewood before long." She turned and smiled, "Come to the table, I have some hot chocolate for my wood toting husband." We sat at our butcher-block table in "Donna's chairs", the few items from her Colorado apartment that made it to Texas. We silently watched the freezing rain make rivulets down the dining room windows. They were the same windows I shattered on the first day we were on the property. I tried to use a long pipe to strike at a snake slithering out of the attic. I missed the snake and broke windows instead.

These past months had been difficult, but we had finished some lucrative work. Donna barely touched her cocoa, taking only little sips. Lost in her thoughts, she stared out at the dark leafless trees. Our afternoon plan was to keep the fire going, put on our PJs, read and have a bowl of mouth-watering, home-made, chicken soup. Later, I watched Donna curl up on the other end of the couch in a blanket. She grasped her second cup of hot chocolate with both hands and held it under her nose, hypnotized by the fire's glowing embers. I smiled at her and whispered, "Thank you. Thank you for believing in me. I love you." She glanced at me, and said, "I love you." Then her eyes returned to the beckoning fireplace. I stared into the glowing coals and thought about the past months. I had resigned from the college, sold art at our first art show, bought a country property, sold the Snyder property, moved and worked hard to open our studio/gallery. We had pushed ourselves and our money to the brink. We had been as exhausted as our finances were. Failure forced us to create a plan that proved that we could do anything. I added a log to the fireplace, Donna was blissfully asleep. I covered her with a quilt and settled back into the couch and whispered to myself, **"I am an artist. I Am a Real Artist"** (Figure 28).

Figure 28: Double Hearts: on all my art since 1973

"Knowledge is only potential power. It becomes power only when, and if, it is organized into definitive plans of action, and directed to a definite end."
Mr. Hill

40 Years as an Artist

A memoir is a reflective remembrance of life. My purpose in writing this memoir is to entertain and inspire. If you enjoyed the stories and created a mental image of this artist's journey from earning a dime to becoming prosperous, then I've completed the first goal. If you've also been inspired to strengthen your commitment to reach new goals, then I've nailed the second goal.

I looked back on my checkered past. Many people said that this little engine (me) could not... In high school a counselor told me, "Lots of geologists are graduating now, I don't think you should consider a career in geology." The following year I won a science fair blue ribbon for my exhibit of personally collected fossils. I was invited to lunch as a special guest of the Petroleum Club. Today, I am an enthusiastic amateur paleontologist. I still collect fossils.

I was told I was too small to go out for sports. In college, I became a trophy winning weightlifter and foil fencer. At Texas Tech, I lifted my weight plus 32 more pounds over my head. In fencing I won 8 matches, until I met Zorro's little brother. The match was over and I won the second-place trophy (Figure 29).

Figure 29: This sketch was on a letter I sent my parents informing them of winning a weightlifting competition

I am 5' 3 1/2" tall, too short by half an inch to be a Marine. I joined and told the drill instructor that I would grow. I went through boot camp and combat training and spent six years in the USMC reserves.

My senior college English teacher told me, "Warren, you can't type, or spell plus you're a poor writer. You're mostly a "C" student, so don't think about a Master's degree program." Years later, I was informed that I have dyslexia. I don't spell but I can draw. That makes up for any misspellings, plus now I have spell check. Who's laughing now?

The first job out of college, Mother asked, "Why are you working at an agency for such a meager salary?" I needed a start. Later that "little pay" proved successful. Napoleon Hill wrote to always give more than is necessary to accomplish the job. I used the commercial artist experience to be hired as an advertising manager at their 5th year entry level.

My family was proud of me, until I walked off the job and moved to Mexico to study art. When I returned from Mexico with an MFA, I was told that my foreign degree would never be acceptable for a teaching position at any college in the U.S.A.. I taught for three years at a university and five years at a college with the master's degree from Institute de Allende in San Miguel de Allende, Guanajuato, Mexico. I was told by "well-meaning folks" that I could never overcome my obstacles to personal and financial success. They were wrong! That old financial goal I pinned to the wall? It took me a little over five years. I continue to increase my prosperity today and into the future.

I am half artist and half business man. I quickly learned that to be a professional artist I had to wear two hats. My art and wallet needed to balance. In observing Dad, an honest business man, I imitated his easy sales approach, and learned his positive one liners, e.g. "Get the facts before you act." I learned to successfully use Dad's wisdom and work ethics. He gave me Napoleon Hill's book, *Think and Grow Rich,* and promised me that if I studied the book, discovered the secrets within and applied them, I would be successful. I did as I was instructed. Napoleon Hill's philosophy on how to think and grow rich worked and is still working today. In college, I studied architectural design and later designed work spaces. As a commercial artist, I learned to create brochures and business cards. As an advertising manager, I learned how to promote products. Bud Biggs taught me how to paint professionally.

Figure 30: Trade House in Beulah, Colorado watercolor

He influenced my decision to resign an eight-year college teaching position in 1976 to make a living as an artist. My business mentor, Percy Harris, taught me the power of being debt free and the purchasing power of cash.

You already know what family and friends said to me, "Warren, you can't make a living as an artist." Brother told me, "You're crazy, have you lost your mind?" Mother was worried "I don't think you can earn enough to support the two of you. Donna will have to find a job." I never did convince Mother we were earning a good living from workshops and painting sales. The last year at the college, my salary was $13,000. The second year as a full-time artist selling art and holding a few watercolor workshops, we earned $28,000.

Dad taught me how to barter. In1980 I traded 54 framed watercolors painted over a five-year period for a three-bedroom house in Beulah, Colorado (Figure 30). Some of my art trades have included: horses, a small sail boat, land, carpet, furniture, jewelry and construction materials. Add to this list, Indian artifacts, pest control services, glasses, dental, doctor and chiropractor services. If you like my art, bring something to trade and we can have some fun bartering.

Past into Present

In 1981 our country art gallery was a pretty place, but the Bertram location without business traffic was a slow declining business. Our income came from traveling to art shows, workshops, and demonstrations.

After five years Donna wanted to move to Austin, so we sold the Bertram property for a good profit and moved. The beautiful three acres had shriveled to a view of an apartment complex parking lot. Donna didn't want to travel with me to art shows anymore so she found a low paying job. I could do the work alone, but I sorely missed her.

During the next year, Donna changed. She became quiet and didn't say much. She acted as if nothing were wrong, but the key to her soul was padlocked, never to reopen. She was there, only in body. I said, "What are we going to do? I feel like you're not here, not participating in our marriage. Do you want to leave or get a divorce?" She simply said, "That's a good idea." She never did say why she wanted a divorce. She became very distant and absent.

Ten years before, in Santa Fe, the night Donna and her friend walked into the bar, I had instantly fallen in love for the first time. Married happily, we never had any anger between us. Now we lived together, but she was missing... vacant. I had planned a two-week workshop at our "Art Trade House" in Colorado and was packing for that trip. Donna showed me how to operate a new answering machine so she would have the time and space to move out. The morning I was to leave she insisted that we make love. I felt I was receiving mixed signals. I drove to Beulah, Colorado thinking that with a little time she would want to work on our marriage.

When I got home, I opened the door to silence. Sweet Donna was gone. I wept. She had kept her word and had taken only a few things; the bed, the TV, and several watercolors. For six weeks, I cried, painted and ate out. Existence, during that time was the most painful period of my life. I kept thinking she would come home. She never did. Our divorce was at the court house in the morning. We went to lunch and spent three hours talking. Donna, best friend, best love, was not ever coming home. Weeks later she shacked up with a man named Andrew. The news crushed me.

Friends, Sharon and Ray invited me to move in with them. At 40, I was living in one room on the second floor of a Northwest Austin condo. Everything was packed in banker boxes stacked head high. I had a bed, a desk and watercolor table. Expenses and responsibilities were few. I was heartbroken and felt I was at the bottom of a well looking up. A friend suggested a meditation class to help cope with my depression. Meditation relaxes mind and body. I began a serious study of the metaphysical. I would prove to myself and to Donna that I could make major money in the art business. Producing watercolors from am to pm, day in day out, I became a painting machine. I turned out one to two paintings a day. I poured all my soul into art. I traveled to more art shows and quadrupled my sales. A year later, in 1982, I bought my current home.

One morning in the process of warming up, I painted over a watercolor from my discard stack. I finished it in 45 minutes. I truly believe the painting was a gift from a higher power. My hand just moved the brush and color around. The painting is an abstract profile of an Indian (Figure 31).

Figure 31: Magic Man (The Magic of Art)

The title "Magic Man" was bestowed on the painting because of the magical way it appeared. This painting changed my direction and outlook on life. It was published as a signed and numbered print. The image size was 26" x 19". The edition selling price started at $75 and moved up quickly. The last 100 numbers of the 750 images sold for $500 each. The last few numbers sold for $950 each. The edition sold out over a period of years for a quarter of a million dollars' profit.

Figure 32: Warren painting at Machu Picchu, Peru, 1984

In 1988, I created a plan along with collectors to sell paintings and prints in five levels of investment, "art futures". The presentation took only 17 minutes during seven dinner parties, with 12 couples in attendance at each dinner. In seven presentations I raised $88,500 on art that I had not yet painted. For six months, I traveled the Southwest, painting the promised inventory. I returned, finished; framed the paintings and held a major opening with 300 people in attendance. Each collector received their chosen art work. A year later, I designed an 840-sq. ft. painting studio, a framing studio, a storage building and greenhouse. All spaces were finished and paid for. The business continued to grow. I paid off my home and was totally debt free.

Figure 33: Warren and a Piaroa native, Southern Venezuela, 1990

I earned enough to join scientific expeditions. Using my drawing and painting skills I went on expeditions to: Machu Picchu, Peru, Easter Island, Spain, Brazil and Venezuela (Figures 32 and 33). My adventures varied, from climbing mountains to fossil collecting in Wyoming with friends Danny Robinson and James Bollmeyer. I sailed with friend Bill Oliver and three other men 600 miles across the South China Sea in a thirty-two-foot boat from Hong Kong to Manila (Figure 34). These waters are the most pirated waters on the high seas.

Selling at art shows is an easy place to meet pretty women. I had many pillow friends (that's what Mother called them). Secretly, I wanted to meet someone like Donna. After being single for sixteen years, I got tired of sleeping with every pretty woman I met. I asked God to make me a happy single man or a happily married person.

At the Fall Art Party in October of 1995 I met Katheryn (Kitty) Louise Biel. She came with her office receptionist and bought a watercolor of "Autumn Leaves". We became friends, then slowly friendship turned into love. Our unity is wonderful, but so different from what Donna and I had. Love is different this time. Love is a deeper and equal partnership with clear communication and understanding. Now is the best part of my life.

On Valentine's day 1999, we married in our back garden, Kitty moved in with her Baby Grand Piano. It filled the small living room. After a year, we got tired of looking at each other through the piano legs. We built a piano room, a second-floor CPA and travel office for Kitty and a double car garage with a circular drive. We named the garage, "Gallarage", because by backing out the cars from the carpeted garage, it becomes an art gallery.

Figure 34: Warren sailing the South China Sea, 1992

We work strongly and have lived happily for the past 20+ years on half of what we have earned. Today, we are still totally debt free and pay very little interest. I was successful when I met Kitty, but she added so much more to my bottom line. She is brilliant. Together we are a great mastermind team, combining business and marriage. We have created an unconventional, exciting life. We live in the other's shadow. Both of us came into the marriage debt free with a little cash. We did not inherit any money or property. We started building our relationship and home by creating a financial plan. We saved, then invested. We are financially conservative. When we purchase, we look for sales. Kitty still clips coupons.

The home I purchased in 1982 was 1,850 square feet (Figure 35). Today with three studios and all the additions we have over 5,000 square feet (Figure 36). We use every square foot of our spacious living and working spaces. Our landscaped one-acre property has a dozen large oak trees in the heart of Austin, Texas.

Figure 35: Cullar residence, Austin, Texas

Figure 36: Cullar Studios, Austin, Texas

I have been a professional artist for over 40 years. I am passionate about my art and it still sells. I have sold art work on time, for over thirty years. I ask for a little down and postdated checks or card slips for the full amount. Having accounts receivable allows me freedom from thinking about money. I call it "mail box money". Money comes from a variety of sources. Kitty has her own CPA practice and travel franchise with Cruise Planners (an American Express Travel Agency) in her "tree top" office upstairs. We cherish our family and friends and live each day with appreciation and thanksgiving. We give back, especially to young artists who cross our threshold to become apprentices for a day or a lifetime. The newest adventure is writing. We published the first book in 2004, *Sketch Book* (On Amazon as an EBook). The sketches from the book were sold to pay for the publishing. Books number three and four are almost ready. In 2000, Kitty persuaded me to take my first cruise as our honeymoon. Now over 65 cruises later, cruising is part of our lives. We have been fortunate to enjoy the world and we spend about three months a year in travel.

Figure 37: "Kitty On Deck" enjoying a cup of coffee

I salute Dad for his spiritual philosophy, mentorship and for being a great father. Napoleon Hill's *Think and Grow Rich* book was my guide to create beyond myself. I salute artist friend and mentor Bud Biggs who challenged me to become a full-time artist. Percy Harris a retired CFO took the time to meet with me once a week for three years to show me how to improve my financial worth. All their influence is ongoing.

This morning from the screened porch, I am typing and enjoying the fall colors. A gust of wind dislodges the yellow leaves of the Elm trees and sprinkles them like rain drops on the emerald Rye grass. Our back landscaped garden and trees are beautiful this October morning.

I take the last sip of coffee and give thanks for Dad, Mr. Hill, Bud and Percy, but especially Kitty. My wonderful wife, best friend, great lover, brilliant CPA, cruise planner, perfect art critic, classical piano player, fun travel companion, excellent chef and heavenly spiritual partner.

PS: Thank you for reading and pass on what you've learned about life to others. If you will excuse me, I will close and return to the studios to create yet one more work of art the world has never seen.

"From the Little Engine that Did"
(Warren Cullar)

Figure 38: Warren and Kitty

"That's All Folks"

The End

1/2/2018

Special Acknowledgements

I have two groups to pay my sincere respects. Those who have proceeded us into spirit and those of us who are waiting for our bus to join them in the future. In writing this book, I remember how *Bud Biggs* called me "Little Brother" and strongly suggested I "don't wait" to paint full time. Bud, bless you for your creative instruction so I could paint for a living.

Donna L. Richards for believing in me to become an artist, pushing me off into a sea everyone told me I would not survive. I did survive in the art, but sadly you did not. Bless you for your loving and caring so long ago.

Percy Harris another of my same size men who taught me the difference between an asset and a liability. Your ability to teach me how to create money and make it work has lead me successfully all these years. Thank you and bless you Percy.

Bill Oliver, creative adventurous friend who believed in me as a spiritual channel and got me to risk more than I thought possible. Thanks Bill for getting me to raise my hand to opportunities I thought were way beyond my level. We talked so much about future lives in spirit. Now, bless you, enjoy your new life in spirit.

A warm and sincere thank you to those who have graciously given of their talents and time. You have given fully with the satisfaction of creating which, in my opinion, is the finest reward one can earn. Yes, each gets compensated in some monetary way but that is not what stirs the heart to produce the creative release that all have, yet few ever allow to flourish.

My wife *Kitty Biel* is the number one candidate to receive the award of appreciation. She has been patient with me, long after patience should have been tested. She has tirelessly assisted this artist who doesn't speak computer. In my art world I hum, in the technological world I fizzle. A million "Thank You's" and "I love You's" would not be enough. I do appreciate, love and bless you Kitty.

My long-time friend *Danny Robinson* (the Major from Africa) for the psychological counseling (He has papers for this work) and for being our "in house" computer geek. Bless you for your warm smile and friendly attitude toward life.

I especially appreciate his bride *Abigayle Lawrence* who came late to the party, picked up the ball and finished an excellent job of editing. Bless you for rescuing me from the tangle of words I had woven.

Brian "Huc" Huculak, a man of many, many talents. I suggested a couple of ideas to Brian and he created an excellent, eye-catching, cover. He can do anything from Landscape Architecture, being an excellent chef, and a lion tamer in Africa with a big camera. He put my old photographs, sketches, and book text into his magic pot and made the ingredients into the meat and potatoes of a good book. Bless you for your long hours and your wide swath of creative skills.

To *Dr. Cathy Chapman* who is first in line to offer encouragement to me to keep on keeping on and to write more books. She has the skills to format the book from my first words to orchestrating the print on demand book and EBook. Bless you for your loving and positive spiritual attitude, it will win any contest.

Although not in this round of book making but the previous 67,000 word book that he assisted with every word for months is *Jacob Pousland*. Another editor chopped up our book into three books, so we started over, hence this book and two more in the wings. Bless you Jacob for showing me how to become a writer.

I noticed the way all have given and cooperated to produce this book. It's all about bringing to the table each one's talents, then sharing, improving and communicating ideas. Although the work is still work, it is the manner in which I recognize that all feel a part of making this adventure come to life. I thank you.

Another group, and it's a big group, who have contributed a pat on the back, given words of encouragement or a passing positive comment. Friend from Boy Scouts, *David Stevenson* (professional writer), who suggested my writing might be better served as a memoir. At that time, I couldn't even spell memoir much less think about writing one.

Then there are folks like my cigar smoking friend *Keith Douglas*, who has kidded me about my writing until I am laughing at myself to the point of tears.

These are only a few of the army of supporters:

- *Carol Ikard*
- *JD Moore*
- *Danielle Hartman Acee*
- *Sally Fitzpatrick*
- *Ceale & Bob Kirkham*
- *Russ Adams*

- *Phillip Auth*
- *Nancy Goedeke*
- *Margie & John Glissmeyer*
- *Lena Rippstein*
- *Larry Davis*
- *John Merriam*
- *Jerry Gatlin*
- *Heather Baxter*
- *David Hammond*
- *Jon Hatcher*
- *Robyn Conley*
- *Becka Oliver*
- *Jennifer Ziegler*
- *Mary Braselton*
- *James Cansler*

And to you, my readers. This work would not be fulfilled without you to pass on what you have learned and to encourage others.

Author & Artist, Warren Cullar

Figure 39: Warren Cullar • Sculptor, Painter, Writer, Traveler

Warren Cullar has been a professional fine artist for over forty years. He is the author of *Sketch Book* consisting of 70 sketches and drawings with a brief statement of where and how the sketches developed. This book, *YES*

You Can Make Money as an Arti$t, is a creative non-fiction memoir. He has two other books in progress, *The Quiet Journey,* is a daily devotional from a metaphysical view point and *My Dad, Napoleon and Me,* is a motivational narrative. As an artist, he creates in a variety of mediums. They include ink line drawings, watercolor and acrylic painting, lithography, soft ground etchings, serigraphs, ceramics and cast bronze sculpture. Traveling is part of his world with 49 stamps in his passport, gathered from cruising, adventure and scientific expeditions. Warren travels the world with a sketch book and watercolors to record his impressions of the cultures and landscapes he encounters. Today, Warren and Kitty, (who has a dual career as an independent CPA and Cruise Planner / Travel Agent) live and work from their spacious home, two studios and sculpture garden in Austin, Texas. You can find Kitty working in her tree top office on the second floor and Warren creating in his sculpture or painting studios.

Discover my webpage: www.artwarren.com

Email me: wcullar@gmail.com

Visit my Blog: "An Artist Who Thinks He Can Write"

You may find my other books on Amazon

53387577R00085

Made in the USA
Columbia, SC
16 March 2019